DK EYEWITNESS TRAVEL

TOP 10
BUDAPEST

D0522460

Top 10 Budapest Highlights

The Top 10 of Everything

CONTENTS

Budapest
Area by Area

Streetsmart

Within each Top 10 list in this book, no hierarchy of quality or popularity is implied. All 10 are, in the editor's opinion, of roughly equal merit.

Front cover and spine *Fishermen's Bastion and Mátyás Church, on the Danube*
Back cover *Chain Bridge, illuminated*
Title page *Statue of Stephen I of Hungary at the Fishermen's Bastion*

The information in this DK Eyewitness Top 10 Travel Guide is checked regularly. Every effort has been made to ensure that this book is as up-to-date as possible at the time of going to press. Some details, however, such as telephone numbers, opening hours, prices, gallery hanging arrangements and travel information, are liable to change. The publishers cannot accept responsibility for any consequences arising from the use of this book, nor for any material on third-party websites, and cannot guarantee that any website address in this book will be a suitable source of travel information. We value the views and suggestions of our readers very highly. Please write to: Publisher, DK Eyewitness Travel Guides, Dorling Kindersley, 80 Strand, London WC2R 0RL, UK, or email travelguides@dk.com

Welcome to
Budapest

Bestriding the Danube, Hungary's capital is not one city but two. Buda, with its medieval streets and imperial palaces, rises on the right bank; Pest, the commercial and political hub of modern Hungary, lines the left. Together they make up what is perhaps one of Europe's finest urban landscape. With Eyewitness Top 10 Budapest, it's yours to explore.

A UNESCO World Heritage Site, Buda's **Castle District** is where both the city and Hungary itself began. The **Royal Palace**, which houses the **National Gallery**, and the historic **Mátyás Church** are just two reminders of the city's importance as a centre of both the Habsburg Empire and of Christianity. More than once the city was Christendom's final bastion against the Ottomans. The opulent Byzantine **Rudas Baths** and **Veli Bej Bath** – which predate the famous **Gellért Baths** by three centuries – are evidence that, on occasion, the Ottomans won. Much of Buda can be explored on foot, while a network of funiculars, historic trains and chairlifts offer access to the many charms of the rolling **Buda Hills** beyond.

When the **Chain Bridge** was completed in 1849, linking Buda and Pest for the first time, the heart of the city shifted from one bank of the Danube to the other. Since then, Pest has become the city's dynamic heart, not least in the lively central shopping and entertainment district around **Váci utca**.

Whether you're visiting for a weekend or longer, our Top 10 guide covers the best of everything the city has to offer, from the grandeur of **Buda** to the bustle of **Pest**. It gives you tips throughout, from finding out what's free to seeking out the best restaurants, along with six easy-to-follow itineraries designed to tie together a clutch of sights in a short space of time. Add inspiring photography and detailed maps, and you've got the essential pocket-sized travel companion. **Enjoy the book, and enjoy Budapest.**

Clockwise from top: **Interior of the Hungarian National Museum; carvings on the Fishermen's Bastion; interior of the Hungarian State Opera; Danube façade of the Hungarian Parliament; statue of a lion on Chain Bridge; Hungarian lace; Centenary Monument on Margaret Island**

Exploring Budapest

Budapest is packed with things to see and do so. Whether you have just a couple of days to explore it or more time, you'll want to make every minute count. To help you do just that, here are two sightseeing itineraries covering the main highlights of Hungary's fascinating capital city.

Fishermen's Bastion, set high on Castle Hill, offers the best view of the city from its conical turrets.

Two Days in Budapest

Day ❶
MORNING
Ride the **Castle Hill Funicular** (see p49) up to the Castle District and stroll the grounds of the **Royal Palace** (see p69) before seeing the fantastic collection of Secession art at the **Hungarian National Gallery** (see pp26–9).
AFTERNOON
Explore medieval Buda: pretty **Lords' Street** (see p70), **Mátyás Church** (see pp30–31) and the ruined **Church of St Mary Magdalene** (see p71). Don't miss views across the Danube from the **Fishermen's Bastion** (see p70).

Day ❷
MORNING
Spend some time in the **Hungarian National Museum** (see pp34–5) before strolling along **Váci utca** (see pp18–19).
AFTERNOON
Take a guided tour of the **Hungarian Parliament** (see pp12–13) and visit **St Stephen's Basilica** (see pp16–17). Afterwards, watch a show at the **Hungarian State Opera** (see pp32–3).

Key
— Two-day itinerary
— Four-day itinerary

Four Days in Budapest

Day ❶
MORNING
Visit **Margaret Island** (see p22–3), a peaceful park situated in the middle of the Danube. Be sure not to miss the Japanese Garden.
AFTERNOON
Explore the Castle District, especially **Lords' Street** (see p70) and **Mátyás Church** (see pp30–31), and enjoy the views from the **Fishermen's Bastion** (see p70). Spend the evening relaxing at the **Gellért Baths** (see pp20–21).

Day ❷
MORNING
Enjoy coffee and pastries at **Gerbeaud Cukrászda** (see p57) on Vörösmarty Square before strolling along **Váci utca** (see pp18–19). Don't miss the **Inner City Parish Church** (see p44).

The Royal Palace, or Castle, is home to several museums, including the world-class Hungarian National Gallery.

time to spare, the **Museum of Applied Arts** *(see p90)*, in a gorgeous Secessionist building, is worth a visit.

Day ❸
MORNING
Stroll along the Pest embankment to the **Hungarian Parliament** *(see pp12–13)*, pausing at the memorial to the massacre of Jews here in January 1945 *(see p48)*. Afterwards, explore the lovely **St Stephen's Basilica** *(see pp16–17)*.
AFTERNOON
The **Great Synagogue** *(see pp36–7)* and its Jewish History Museum are a must-see. After your visit, take a tour of the **Hungarian State Opera** *(see pp32–3)* and catch an evening performance.

Day ❹
MORNING
Start your day at the **Royal Palace** *(see p69)*, visiting both the **Hungarian National Gallery** *(see pp26–9)* and the **Budapest History Museum** *(see p69)*.
AFTERNOON
Head into the **Buda Hills** *(see p101)* via the chair lift to the top of **János Hill** *(see p103)*. Take a ride on the unique **Children's Railway** *(see p52)* to the Elizabeth Lookout Tower. Climb to the top for great views of the city.

AFTERNOON
Allow yourself the luxury of a full afternoon to take in all that the superb **Hungarian National Museum** *(see pp34–5)* has to offer. If you have

Top 10 Budapest Highlights

The Grand Staircase of the Hungarian Parliament

🔟 Budapest Highlights

The finest of the Habsburg triumvirate of Budapest, Vienna and Prague, the Hungarian capital is much grander in scale than its counterparts. Comprising two separate towns – hilly Buda on the Danube's western bank and flat Pest on the eastern bank – this is a city rich in historical sights.

1 Hungarian Parliament

Viewed from the opposite bank of the Danube, the façade of the Hungarian Parliament is one of Budapest's defining sights. Its chambers contain magnificent treasures *(see pp12–15).*

2 St Stephen's Basilica

With its 96-m- (315-ft-) high dome visible from all over the city, St Stephen's Basilica houses the city's most bizarre relic – the mummified forearm of St Stephen (King István) *(see pp16–17).*

3 Váci utca

For centuries, Váci utca has been the centre of the Hungarian commercial world, and it remains Budapest's retail and social hub *(see pp18–19).*

4 Gellért Hotel and Baths

Budapest is famous for its numerous thermal baths, and the best are the indoor and outdoor pools at the legendary Gellért Hotel *(see pp20–21).*

5 Margaret Island

Isolated until the 19th century and long a retreat for religious contemplation, the lush and still-secluded Margaret Island is an ideal place for a peaceful stroll *(see pp22–3).*

6 Hungarian National Gallery

The six permanent exhibitions spread throughout much of Budapest's Royal Palace present the most valuable collection of Hungarian art in the world *(see pp26–9)*.

7 Mátyás Church

The coronation church of the Hungarian kings, with its Gothic spire towering above much of Upper Buda, is as impressive close up as it is from afar *(see pp30–31)*.

Margit híd
Margaret Bridge

Duna (Danube)

ÚJPESTI RAKPART

ID. ANTALL JÓZSEF RKPT

PÁK MIKSA U

SZENT ISTVÁN KÖRÚT

POZSONYI U

DÓZSA ERNŐ U

CSÁNÁDY U

HEGEDŰS GYULA U

VISEGRÁDI U

VÁCI U.

ANGELO ROTTA RKPT

MARKÓ U

NYUGATI TÉR

KOSSUTH LAJOS TÉR

ALKOTMÁNY U

PODMANICZKY U

TERÉZVÁROS

TERÉZ KÖRÚT

NAGYMEZŐ U

BAJCSY-ZSILINSZKY ÚT

SZABADSÁG TÉR

BANK U

ARANY JÁNOS U

ANDRÁSSY ÚT

Széchenyi lánchíd
Chain Bridge

Széchenyi
SZÉCHENYI RAKPART

JÓZSEF ATTILA U

JANE HAINING RAKPART

SZÉCHENYI ISTVÁN TÉR

DOROTTYA U

ERZSÉBET TÉR

KIRÁLY U

ERZSÉBETVÁROS

SZÁNYÓ U

DOB U

WESSELÉNYI U

KLAUZÁL U

CLARK ÁDÁM TÉR

FRIEDRICH BORN RKPART

APÁCZAI U

PETŐFI S U

SZERVITA TÉR

KÁROLY KRT

RÁKÓCZI ÚT

KOSSUTH L U

Duna (Danube)

KRISZTINA KÖRÚT

JÓZSEFVÁROS

SZABAD SAJTÓ ÚT

MÚZEUM KRT

BRÓDY SÁNDOR U

SZENTKIRÁLY U

HEGYALJA ÚT

DÖBRENTEI TÉR

Erzsébet híd
Elizabeth Bridge

VÁCI U

SZERB U

SZABADSÁG TÉR

SZÉP U

DÓZSA WALLENBERG RKPT

SZENT GELLÉRT RKPT

VÁMHÁZ KÖRÚT

LÓNYAY U

ÜLLŐI ÚT

RÁDAY U

CSARNOK TÉR

GELLÉRT

Szabadság híd
Liberty Bridge

KÖZRAKTÁR

KINIZSI U

0 metres   500
0 yards   500

8 Hungarian State Opera

Built to rival the opera houses of Vienna and Dresden, the sublime Hungarian State Opera stages world-class performances *(see pp32–3)*.

10 Great Synagogue

The largest of its kind in Europe, Budapest's Great Synagogue was built in 1854–9, in a Byzantine-style design. It also houses the Jewish History Museum *(see pp36–7)*.

9 Hungarian National Museum

A treasure-trove of exhibits and artifacts from every period of Hungary's turbulent history *(see pp34–5)*.

TOP 10 ⭐ Hungarian Parliament

In 1846, the Hungarian poet Mihály Vörösmarty wrote with some desperation that "the motherland has no home". When Hungary opened its magnificent Parliament building after decades of construction in 1902, it not only had a home, but one of the finest Neo-Gothic buildings in Europe. The largest parliament building in the world at the time, it stood as a symbol of Hungarian self-confidence in the early 20th century. Designed by Imre Steindl, it is one of Budapest's defining landmarks, surpassed only by the Royal Palace.

① Cross-Danube Vista
Sensational close up, the Hungarian Parliament is arguably even better from afar. Set along the banks of the Danube **(below)**, its spires and symmetry can be admired from the other side of the river.

② Main Entrance
Inspired by London's Houses of Parliament, and built with no expense spared, the main entrance is guarded by two lions sculpted by Béla Markup and József Somogyi.

③ Crown Jewels
Spirited out of Hungary after World War II – and stored in Fort Knox, USA, until 1978 – the Crown of St Stephen and the Royal Sceptre are now kept in the Domed Hall.

④ National Assembly Hall
The Hungarian Lower House is where Parliament sits. The bullet hole above the lectern dates from 1912, when an assassin tried to kill the speaker, István Tisza.

⑤ Grand Staircase
The sumptuous main staircase **(left)** is decorated with three outstanding ceiling frescoes. These include Károly Lotz's *Glorification of Hungary*, depicting scenes from the lives of the country's kings and saints.

6 Delegation Room

A relic of the Dual Monarchy (see p76), this was where parliamentarians met delegates of the ministries. Its walls have artworks by Andor Dudits, while the ceiling paintings, *Wisdom* and *Fortitude*, are by Károly Lotz.

7 Domed Hall

The spiritual heart of the building, the Domed Hall **(right)** was once used to host joint sessions of Parliament. Each of the 16 pillars supporting the dome features a statue of a Hungarian king or queen (see pp14–15). The hall is used for official ceremonies.

IMRE STEINDL

Before submitting his entry for the competition to design Hungary's Parliament, Imre Steindl also submitted designs for a proposed parliament in Berlin. His plans were rejected, and the winning entry was, of course, Paul Wallot's Reichstag. Berlin's loss was Hungary's gain as Steindl's vision resulted in a masterpiece. He is remembered by a bust, cast by Alajos Stróbl, on the main staircase.

8 The Conquest

The finest work of art here is Munkácsy's *The Conquest*. Originally intended for the Chamber of Commons, it was rejected as it was thought to misrepresent the first contact between the invading Magyars and Pannonian tribes as a peaceful meeting, rather than a heroic conquest.

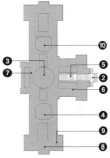

NEED TO KNOW

MAP J1 ▪ V, Kossuth Lajos tér 1–3 ▪ 06 441 49 04; 06 441 44 15 ▪ Dis. access ▪ http://latogatokozpont.parlament.hu/en

Visitor Centre: Apr–Oct: 8am–6pm daily; Nov–Mar: 8am–4pm daily. Go to the visitor centre for more information.

Adm: Ft2,200 for EU residents and Ft5,400 for all others.

▪ The only way to see all the building's attractions is by guided tour when Parliament is not in session.

▪ To book a ticket, call 06 441 49 04 or 06 441 44 15 (English is spoken), or visit the website.

▪ There is no café on the premises, but there is one in the visitor centre, and many more in the surrounding area.

9 Prime Minister's Office

The prime minister's office is closed to visitors, but you can admire its reception rooms, with 1930s paintings by Géza Udvary and Antal Diósy.

10 Congress Hall

Unused for legislation since 1944, when Hungary became a unicameral state, the former Hungarian Upper House **(above)** has a rich interior with a painting by Zsigmond Vajda of the monk Astrik handing St Stephen his crown.

Domed Hall Statues

Statue of Prince Árpád

1 Prince Árpád

Prince Árpád was chosen as the leader of the Magyar tribes shortly after they settled on the Pannonian plains in AD 896. The Magyars migrated from the Ural mountains in present-day Russia.

2 St Stephen

St Stephen (István) was elected Duke of the Magyars in AD 997. He adopted Christianity soon after, and was crowned king by Pope Sylvester II in 1001.

3 St Ladislaus

Hungary's ruler from 1077 to 1095, Ladislaus was victorious against the Turks and the Cumans, and annexed Croatia in 1092.

4 András II

The son of King Béla III and brother of Emeric, András II was crowned in 1205. He greatly expanded the Magyar state eastwards, conquering large swathes of Transylvania and encouraging vast numbers of Magyars to settle in the region.

5 Béla IV

Defeated by the Tatars in 1241, Béla IV survived to rebuild Hungary after the Tatars left the country in ashes a year later. His patient rebuilding of the nation over the next 25 years elevated him to greatness.

6 Louis I

Crowned in 1342, Louis the Great reigned for 40 years, expanding the Magyar kingdom with victories over Venice and Dalmatia between 1357 and 1358. In 1370, he formed a political union with Poland after the death of his uncle, the Polish king Casimir III, and ruled as sovereign of both countries until his death in 1382.

7 János Hunyadi

János Hunyadi was born to a Romanian family of Vlach nobles who had long served the Hungarian king Sigismund. A gifted commander, Hunyadi became the ruler of Transylvania in 1441, and then Governor of Hungary in 1446. He is best remembered for defeating the Turks in the Battle of Belgrade in 1456.

8 Mátyás Corvinus

The second son of János, Mátyás was born in Cluj-Napoca, Transylvania, and is generally considered to be the greatest of all Hungarian kings. Crowned in 1458 at the age of 15, he was a Renaissance man who valued the sciences, arts and architecture, and invited foreign writers, humanists, musicians and

Domed Hall Statues

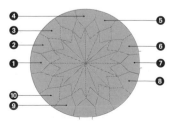

artists to his court. The first Hungarian printing press and library were founded during his 32-year reign.

9 Charles III

In 1687, Hungary finally succumbed to Austrian domination and renounced its right to elect its own king. The Habsburgs inherited the throne and Charles VI, the last Holy Roman Emperor of the direct Habsburg line, became Charles VI King of Bohemia and Charles III King of Hungary. The king spent much of his reign ensuring that his daughter, Maria Theresa, would succeed him.

10 Maria Theresa

Maria Theresa acceded to the throne in 1740, cementing Hungary's position as an integral part of the

Interior of the Domed Hall

Habsburg Empire. Buda became an imperial city and the magnificent Habsburg Royal Palace was built during the Queen's reign. The city became a centre of Central European art, second only to Vienna. Maria ruled Hungary until her death in 1780.

THE DOMED HALL

The first section of the Parliament to be completed was the Domed Hall in 1896. It was used for a special session of Parliament held during Budapest's Millennium Celebrations. The 16-sided dome – which, at 96 m (315 ft), is the same height as that of St Stephen's Basilica – was designed to convey a sense of amplified space. Each of the 16 pillars supporting the dome bears the statue and coat of arms of a significant Hungarian ruler. Apart from the ten dignitaries mentioned above, the six remaining statues represent (in a clockwise direction) Könyves Kálmán, András III, István Báthory, István Bocskai, Gabor Bethlen and Leopold II.

Magnificent ceiling of the domed hall

TOP 10 DATES IN THE PARLIAMENT'S HISTORY

1 1885 Foundation stone laid, 12 Oct

2 1896 First session of Parliament, 15 Mar

3 1902 Parliament building completed

4 1912 Assassin attempts to shoot speaker, 4 Jun

5 1920 Treaty of Trianon strips Hungary of two-thirds of its territory, 4 Jun

6 1944 Hungary becomes a unicameral republic

7 1956 Armed uprising breaks out against Soviet rule, 23 Oct. Soviet tanks intervene and a new government is set up

8 1958 Execution of Prime Minister Imre Nagy, 16 Jun

9 1989 Communists allow multi-party elections, Oct

10 1990 MPs take their seats after post-Communist elections, 2 May

🔟 ⭐ St Stephen's Basilica

More than worthy of St Stephen (see p40), the Basilica that carries his name is visible from all over Budapest. Splendidly lit in the evening, it is perhaps the most photographed sight in the city. The dome, at 96 m (315 ft), is the same height as that of Parliament, whose builders decided not to go higher. It was built between 1851 and 1905 in the form of a Greek cross, and is the work of three architects – József Hild, Miklós Ybl and József Kauser.

5 Main Portal
The colossal oak front door is decorated with medallions that depict the heads of the 12 Apostles. Despite the door's age the carvings remain an impressive sight.

3 Dome and Mosaics
The Neo-Renaissance dome was designed by Miklós Ybl in 1867 after the original dome – designed by József Hild – caved in due to poor workmanship and materials. It is decorated with mosaics **(right)** by Károly Lotz. A viewing platform above the cupola offers panoramic views of the city; it is reached by a lift and stairs.

1 Main Altar
A life-size marble statue of St Stephen (King István), by sculptor Alajos Stróbl, dominates the main altar **(above)** of the Basilica. On either side, fine paintings by the 19th-century artist Gyula Benczúr depict scenes from the saint-king's life.

4 North Tower
The 9,144-kg (9-ton) bell in the North Tower **(below)** was paid for by German Catholics, who were ashamed that the Nazis had looted the original at the end of World War II during their retreat from Budapest. The original bell was never traced.

6 St Gellért and St Emeric
Alajos Stróbl carved the statue of St Gellért and his pupil, St Emeric (St Stephen's son, Imre), that stands in a small nave in the centre of the main hall. Opposite, the statue of St Elizabeth is by Károly Senyei.

2 Main Entrance
"I am the way and the truth and the life" proclaims the Latin inscription above the Basilica's main entrance. Situated above the inscription are several statues of Hungarian saints paying homage to the Virgin Mary and the infant Jesus.

7 Figures of the 12 Apostles
The Basilica's rear colonnade has 12 superb statues by Leó Feszler representing the 12 Apostles. Below is a fine Neo-Classical loggia.

8 Holy Right Hand

The mummified forearm of St Stephen **(left)** is displayed in the Holy Right Hand Chapel near the main altar. It was taken to Dubrovnik in Croatia by Béla IV in the 13th century to protect it from the Tatars. After time in Vienna and at the Royal Palace in Buda, it was brought here on 20 August 1945 – St Stephen's Day.

ORGAN CONCERTS

The Basilica's organ was made by Angster & Sons of Pécs, and installed in 1904. At the time, it was considered the world's finest. The organ was enlarged in 1934, and today comprises no fewer than 5,898 pipes. You can hear it at special organ concerts, which are held in the Basilica from time to time.

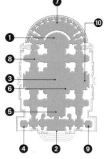

9 Treasury

A replica of the holy Hungarian crown is the centrepiece of a small collection of religious jewellery. The original crown is now kept in the Hungarian Parliament *(see pp12–15)*. Gifts to Hungarian kings from a succession of popes are also on display.

10 Gyula Benczúr Painting

The painting *St Stephen*, by Gyula Benczúr, is one of the most important works in the Hungarian artistic cannon. It portrays the king who died without an heir – proffering the care of the country and the crown to the Virgin Mary.

NEED TO KNOW

MAP L2 ▪ V, Szent István tér ▪ 06 317 28 59 ▪ Dis. access ▪ Guided tours: 06 338 21 51; turizmus@basilica.hu

Open 9am–5pm Mon–Fri, 9am–1pm Sat, 1–5pm Sun. Treasury and tower: timings vary. Guided tours: 10am–3pm Mon–Sat

Donations to the main church are welcome but not mandatory. Guided tours: Ft400 (includes Treasury). Dome viewing platform: Ft500

▪ Every year on St Stephen's Day (20 Aug), the Holy Right Hand is carried by the Basilica's priests past large crowds

of people who gather in front of the Basilica. Arrive early to witness the spectacle.

▪ Choose from among a number of restaurants and cafés located opposite the Basilica's main entrance.

TOP 10 ★ Váci utca

Váci utca is one of the city's best-known streets. With two parts – the northern end for shopping and the southern end for drinking and eating – it buzzes with life day and night, and acts as the city's commercial and social hub. Most of the street is pedestrianized apart from where it is bisected by the access road to Elizabeth Bridge. To get a real feel of the street, you should stroll down its full length.

1 Gerbeaud Cukrászda

This is the most famous coffee house in Budapest. Since 1858, Gerbeaud Cukrászda **(above)** has been known for its richly decorated interior *(see p57)*. Expect slow service.

2 Vörösmarty tér Metro Station

The tiled walls, wooden booths and platforms of this immaculate 1903 station remind one why underground railways were considered glamorous. The tiny yellow trains are enchanting too.

3 Philanthia

This Secession-style florists opened in 1905 and now occupies part of the Neo-Classical block at No. 9. The block was built in 1840 by József Hild and was once occupied by the Inn of the Seven Electors, which had a large ballroom/concert hall where a 12-year-old Franc Liszt performed.

4 The Promenade

Walk the full length of Váci utca **(right)** from Vörösmarty tér to Vámház körút and on your way take in the atmosphere, the bustle and the stunning architecture of the street's buildings. You won't be alone during the summer, but the crowds are a part of the appeal.

6 Thonet House

Built from 1888 to 1890 by Ödön Lechner and Gyula Pártos, Thonet House once belonged to a wealthy family. Zsolnay ceramics **(left)** adorn the walls, while the shop sells exclusive crystal.

5 Klotild Palaces

Forming a splendid entrance to Elizabeth Bridge, the twin Klotild Palaces **(below)** were commissioned by Archduchess Klotild, daughter-in-law of Emperor Franz József, and finished in 1902. Their interiors are mostly shops or offices. They also house the luxurious Buddha-Bar Hotel *(see p115)*.

7 St Michael's City Church

First built around 1230, St Michael's City Church **(left)** was devastated by the Turks in 1541, rebuilt in 1701 and renovated between 1964 and 1968. Its plain exterior belies a rich interior, including a fine gold pulpit and dome.

> **VÁCI UTCA**
>
> The name of Budapest's famous street has simple origins. The street was once the main road linking Pest to the town of Vác *(see p65)*, 40 km (25 miles) north of Budapest. The gate leading to Vác used to stand at Váci utca No. 3.

8 Herendi Márkabolt

Herendi ceramics are famous for their intricacy and quality. This outlet is one of the few places you can be sure of finding the genuine article.

9 Central Market Hall

Budapest's largest market has innumerable stalls on the ground floor selling vegetables, fish and cheese. Specialities are spicy *kolbász* salami and sheep's cheese. The upper-level stalls sell local crafts *(see p59)*.

10 1000 Tea

Váci utca has lots of places to eat, drink and while away the hours, but a relaxing oasis away from the hustle and bustle is 1000 Tea. This quiet café has a selection of loose leaf teas from all over the world. It is a great place to rest after a day's shopping.

NEED TO KNOW

MAP C4-C5

Gerbeaud Cukrászda: V, Vörösmarty tér 7; 06 429 90 00; www.gerbeaud.hu; 9am–9pm daily

Philanthia: Váci utca 9; 0670 933 22 66

Thonet House: Váci utca 11

Herendi Márkabolt: Kígyó utca 5; 06 266 63 05; 10am–7pm daily

1000 Tea: Váci utca 65; 06 337 82 17

■ Beware of pickpockets operating the length of Váci utca. Also watch out for attractive women inviting men for drinks on this street – the men are often left with extremely overpriced bar tabs to pay at the end of the night.

■ Most places here can be expensive, and some have dubious pricing policies. Make sure prices are clearly indicated on the menu and check your bill carefully.

Map of Váci utca

Gellért Hotel and Baths

The Gellért Baths is the finest of all the great bath houses in Budapest. Its main swimming pool is perhaps the best example of Neo-Classical architecture in Hungary, and is certainly the ideal place to enjoy Budapest's warm therapeutic waters. The hotel itself is a fine Secessionist piece, designed by Ármin Hegedűs, Artúr Sebestyén and Izidor Sterk, and built between 1912 and 1918. It was damaged by heavy bombing in World War II and rebuilt in the late 1940s.

1 Façade
The Gellert's Secession-era façade **(below)** reflects the self-confidence of the era in which it was constructed – during the final phase of the Habsburg Empire, when Hungary was poised on the verge of independence.

2 Main Entrance Hall
With elaborate mosaics and over-the-top statues, the hotel's entrance hall is a leap into the past. The staff are patient with visitors who just want to admire the scene.

3 Main Staircase
The stained-glass windows **(right)** on the staircase landings were designed by Bózó Stanisits. They illustrate a legend about a magic stag, recorded in János Arany's poetry.

4 Main Swimming Pool
The stunning Neo-Classical main pool **(above)** is the finest part of the Gellért baths. Surrounded by high galleries and marble columns, it is decorated with colourful mosaics. Note that it is obligatory to wear a swimming cap in this part of the baths.

5 Panorama Restaurant and Terrace
There's no better place to enjoy a hearty and relaxed Sunday brunch in Budapest than on the well-shaded, first-floor restaurant of the Gellért Hotel. The views from here over the Danube and the city to the castle and Fishermen's Bastion are simply magnificent.

7 Gellért Eszpresszó

This is an old-fashioned coffee and teahouse with a mouthwatering range of cakes and pastries. You are served by liveried waitresses, and the Viennese-style furniture adds to the splendour of the place.

8 Eastern-Style Towers

Although the Gellért is primarily a Secessionist building, its cylindrical, Eastern-style towers commemorate the earlier Turkish baths that stood on this site.

Thermal Baths 9

The medicinal waters here were first discovered in the 13th century during the reign of King András II. In the Middle Ages, a hospital was built on this spot. Today, there is a great network of thermal baths **(right)** at various temperatures. Massages and baths with medical services are available.

HEALING WATERS

Although Budapest is known for its baths, few visitors realize the major role they play in city life, and how much faith the locals place in the healing properties of their waters. For many of the city's older residents, the baths remain as important as they were under the Ottomans, who first developed the potential of Budapest's astonishing 120-odd thermal springs. Most of the city's thermal waters contain high levels of sulphur, and are said to be especially effective in treating rheumatism, arthritis and even Parkinson's disease.

6 Bath Foyers

There are three foyers at the entrance. The central foyer's glass roof is the highlight, but the floors, walls, statuettes and benches of the others are also marvellous. You can admire them without paying to enter the baths.

10 Outdoor Pools

During the summer, bathers head to the outdoor pools and sun terraces. The main outdoor pool was one of the first in the world to have an artificial wave mechanism, which is still in use today.

NEED TO KNOW

MAP L6

Danubius Hotel Gellért: XI, Szent Gellért tér 1; 06 889 55 00; www.danubius hotels.com/gellert

Gellért Baths: XI, Kelen-hegyi út 4; 06 466 61 66; Dis. access; www.budapest spas.hu; 6am–8pm daily

Adm Ft5,100 weekdays, Ft5,300 weekends (lockers are cheaper than cabins; also cheaper within 3 hours of closing)

Panorama Restaurant & Terrace: noon– midnight summer, 7pm–midnight winter, closed Mon

Gellért Eszpresszó: 9am–8pm

■ Swimming costumes and towels can be hired at the baths but are costly, so it's best to bring your own.

■ Standard entry at Gellért includes access to the baths, swimming pool, sauna and steam room. Special treatments incur an additional cost.

TOP 10 ⭐ Margaret Island

Inhabited since Roman times, Margaret Island (Margitsziget) is a tranquil, green oasis in the middle of the Danube. It is named after Princess Margit, daughter of King Béla IV, who spent most of her life in the island's convent in the 13th century. It was also a popular hunting ground for medieval kings. The island has served as Budapest's playground since 1869.

2 Franciscan Church

The secluded ruins of the 14th-century Franciscan church **(left)** lie in the island's centre. Though there is very little left to admire, it still has a fine arched window and a staircase.

3 St Michael's Church

The oldest building on Margaret Island, St Michael's Church was founded in the 11th century, but was devastated by the Turks in 1541. Visitors today can see a 1930s reconstruction, which used materials salvaged from the original building.

1 Dominican Convent

One of the island's most important monuments is the ruin of a 13th-century Dominican convent. This was founded by Béla IV, whose daughter Margit came to live here in 1251. A plaque in the church marks the spot where she is buried.

4 Centenary Monument

The striking Modernist Centenary Monument **(left)** was installed in 1973 to commemorate the unification of Buda, Óbuda and Pest to form Budapest in 1873.

5 Japanese Garden

The most delightful spot on the island is the Japanese Garden **(below)** at the northern end, with lily pools, rock gardens and waterfalls.

NEED TO KNOW

MAP B1 ■ Margaret Island (Margitsziget): Budapest XIII

■ The easiest way to get to Margaret Island is by bus No. 26 from Nyugati Station. However, the most enjoyable way is by boat. In summer, public transport boats marked D13 run along the Danube stopping twice at the island, near the Centenary Monument and the hotels in the north. Check the timetable at bkk.hu/en.

■ For lunch, head to Palatinus Strand for *lángos* (fried salty dough with toppings) and hot dogs. For a formal meal, visit the Danubius Grand Hotel Margitsziget.

6 Water Tower

The UNESCO-protected Water Tower (below), built in 1911, also serves as an exhibition hall during the summer season. It stands 57 m (187 ft) high, and a gallery offers panoramic views of the island.

8 Musical Fountain

From March to October, this fountain leaps into action morning and night, shooting water in time to a classical piece or pop song. Coloured lights are added for evening performances.

PRINCESS MARGIT (MARGARET)

After the horrors of the Mongol invasion and subsequent destruction of Budapest from 1241 to 1242, a desperate King Béla IV offered to give his daughter to God if, in return, He would ensure that the Mongols never returned. In 1251, Béla made good his vow and sent his 9-year-old daughter Margit to the island's convent, where she stayed for the rest of her life. The Mongols never returned.

Map of Margaret Island

10 Bodor Well

The unusual musical Bodor Well (below) is a copy of a long-destroyed well, built in 1820 in Târgu Mures, Romania. This copy dates from 1936, and plays recorded music on the hour.

7 Palatinus Strand

Opened in 1919, the city's largest outdoor pool complex buzzes from dawn to dusk, as people enjoy the therapeutic waters pumped from the island's thermal springs (see p47). There are water slides and special pools for the kids.

9 Danubius Grand Hotel Margitsziget

This legendary hotel designed by Miklós Ybl opened in 1872. For years, it was the most fashionable in the city, attracting aristocracy from all over Europe. Today, it has been joined by a sister spa (see p47).

Following pages The Chain Bridge over the Danube

TOP 10 ⊛ Hungarian National Gallery

The treasure-trove that is the Hungarian National Gallery has been housed in the Royal Palace since 1975, when a large section of the building was given over to it. It displays pieces from medieval times to the present day, and there are six permanent exhibitions that present the cream of Hungarian fine arts. The Gallery's collection is shared with the Museum of Fine Arts *(see p95)*, and is especially strong in Secession art *(see p29)*.

1 The Recapture of Buda Castle in 1686
Gyula Benczúr painted this masterpiece **(below)** for the 1896 Millennium Celebrations. It was meant to emphasize the need for Austro-Hungarian rule by showing that Hungary was only freed from Turkish rule thanks to Karl of Lotharingia and Eugene of Savoy.

2 Picnic in May
Painted from memory in 1873 by Pál Szinyei-Merse, *Picnic in May* is close to the French Impressionist style. The figure lying with his back towards us is the artist himself.

3 Women of Eger
Besides his fine portrait work, Bertalan Székely painted historical works featuring simple, heroic female figures in a romantic style. *Women of Eger* (1867), portrays the women of the town defending Eger Castle against the Turks.

4 Habsburg Crypt
This Crypt, with the exquisite sarcophagus of Palatine Archduke Joseph, is a Neo-Classical warren of black-and-white marble and gold leaf. It can only be seen on a guided tour.

5 Great Throne Room
An entire room of the Gallery is devoted to 15th- and 16th-century Gothic altarpieces. The best, painted in 1520, depicts St Anne and St John the Baptist from a church in Kisszeben (Sabinov, in present-day Slovakia).

6 The Visitation
Nothing is known about Master MS, who was the chief exponent of late Gothic painting in Hungary. His best work **(above)**, dated 1500–10, depicts the Virgin Mary meeting St Elizabeth.

7 The Yawning Apprentice
The Yawning Apprentice (1867) **(below)** is a well-known and much-loved work by Hungary's finest Realist, Mihály Munkácsy. It is celebrated for its extraordinary detail.

8 Main Entrance
Part of the 18th-century Maria Theresa Palace, the late Baroque façade has an eclectic range of influences.

Birdsong

Károly Ferenczy was one of Hungary's finest artists at the turn of the 19th century. *Birdsong* **(right)**, painted in 1893, is one of his best works. It sees him move away from the "delicate naturalism" made famous by French artists like Jules Bastien-Lepage and towards his own distinct style.

MIHÁLY MUNKÁCSY

Regarded as Hungary's finest artist, Mihály Munkácsy began his career making finished woodwork. After completing his first major painting in 1869, when he was just 25, he moved to Paris, where he painted a series of masterpieces including *The Churning Woman* and *Woman Carrying Brushwood*, both now in the National Gallery. He died in 1900 at the age of 55 in Paris.

The Visitation ❻

❾ Birdsong

❿ Woman Bathing

❸ Women of Eger

❷ Picnic in May

Key to Floorplan
- Ground floor
- 1st floor
- 2nd floor
- 3rd floor

❺ Great Throne Room

Main Entrance ❽

❹ Habsburg Crypt

❶ The Recapture of Buda Castle in 1686

❼ The Yawning Apprentice

Woman Bathing ❿

Nudes were a speciality of Károly Lotz, who painted this particularly sensuous figure in 1901. A fine example of academic painting, it evokes the style of the French artist, Ingres. Lotz is also known for the murals in the Hungarian Parliament *(see pp12–14)*.

NEED TO KNOW

MAP H4 ■ Buda Castle, Royal Palace buildings A, B, C and D ■ 06 201 90 82; 0620 439 73 31 ■ Dis. access at building A ■ www.mng.hu

Open 10am–6pm Tue–Sun.

Adm Ft1,800; audio guide in English available for select collections, Ft800

■ A free guided tour of the permanent collection is available in English from 2pm every Thursday and 11am every Saturday. For

information and booking, call 06 201 90 82.

■ In 2018, part of the 19th- and 20th-century collections is expected to move to a new gallery building in the Városliget (City Park).

Secession Works in the Gallery

1 Woman in a White-Spotted Dress

József Rippl-Rónai (1861–1927) was one of the three most important artists of the Secession movement. He studied for several years in Paris, at a time when the Art Nouveau movement was starting to flourish. His masterpiece *Woman in a White-Spotted Dress* (1889) depicts the somewhat affected pose of a model apparently caught off-guard. It is said to have been the first Secession-style work painted in Hungary.

Woman in a White-Spotted Dress

2 Woman with a Birdcage

An early painting by Rippl-Rónai, *Woman with a Birdcage* (1892) is renowned for its marvellous use of contrast – note the white of the girl's hands compared to the blurred, dark background. The slightly contrived pose of the model holding the cage is a trademark of the artist.

3 The Manor House at Körtvélyes

Rippl-Rónai visited Italy in 1904 and was fascinated by the decorative mosaics he saw in many homes. This 1907 work anticipates his shift from soft brushwork to bolder strokes, which would culminate in the paintings of his later years.

The Manor House at Körtvélyes

4 Girls Getting Dressed

This 1912 Rippl-Rónai work shows the progression of his characteristic "corn kernels" style, where his brushstrokes became bolder and his colours brighter. The somewhat awkward pose of the girl on the left betrays the artist's love of playing with the viewer's perception.

5 The Golden Age

The second of Hungary's great Secessionist triumvirate, János Vaszary (1867–1939) oscillated between Art Nouveau and Post-Impressionism. His best work is probably this 1898 rendition of a couple yearning for a lost paradise.

Fancy Dress Ball

6 Fancy Dress Ball

Vaszary's brightly coloured 1907 portrayal of Budapest society has a touch of decadence. Notice the man's leer and the licentious pose.

7 Breakfast in the Open Air

This painting by Vaszary makes fabulous use of light and colour. At first glance, it seems to be a sympathetic depiction of Budapest society. Yet the indifference of the girl's parents towards her behaviour could be interpreted as a criticism of societal values at the time.

8 Riders in the Park

Dating from 1919, this is another fine example of late Secessionist painting by Vaszary, with sharp brushstrokes and high contrast colours. The influence of Matisse, whom he knew from his sojourns in Paris, is clearly visible in this work.

9 The Garden of the Magician

Lajos Gulácsy (1882–1932) was the youngest

The Garden of the Magician

of Hungary's famous Secessionist trio. His style and approach were greatly influenced by spending 13 years in Italy, where he painted *The Garden of the Magician*. His output also shows echoes of the English Pre-Raphaelites, particularly the work of Dante Gabriel Rossetti.

10 Self-Portrait with Hat

Lajos Gulácsy's *Self-Portrait with Hat* (1912) reinforces his rather detached view of the world and, perhaps, his lack of belief in his own abilities. In the painting, his face is wearing an anxious and vulnerable expression.

THE SECESSION

From its quiet beginnings among avant-garde artists in Vienna in the late 1880s, until it gave way to Art Deco in the 1920s, the Secession movement was an attempt to break away from the romantic historicism of 19th-century art. It tried to find new inspiration in the distant past; in Hungary it explored the bold colours of Transylvanian folk art. Often characterized by fantastical designs, bright colours and stylized forms, the movement repossessed art from the nationalists. It encompassed all forms of the decorative and visual arts, from painting and sculpture to interior design. It is represented in the paintings of the National Gallery, in the Zsolnay ceramics all round the city and, above all, in the architecture of the day.

TOP 10 SECESSIONIST BUILDINGS

1 Four Seasons Hotel Gresham Palace *(Map K3)*

2 Danubius Gellért Hotel *(Map L6)*

3 Museum of Applied Arts *(Map D5)*

4 Geology Institute *(Map F3)*

5 Hungarian National Bank *(Map K2)*

6 Post Office Savings Bank *(Map L2)*

7 Városliget Calvinist Church *(Map E3)*

8 Franz Liszt Academy of Music *(Map D3)*

9 New York Palace *(Map D4)*

10 New Theatre *(Map M2)*

Gresham Palace is now a hotel, and is famous for its Secessionist stained glass and mosaics *(see p83 & p116)*.

TOP 10 ★ Mátyás Church

The profusion of architectural styles in Mátyás Church reveals the building's and the city's troubled history. The original church was destroyed in 1241 and a new church, part of Béla IV's fortified city, was built from 1255 to 1269. Much of this Gothic building remains, but it was Mátyás Corvinus, the church's namesake, who expanded it in the 15th century. The final phase of restoration took place in 1873–96, when Frigyes Schulek redesigned it in the Neo-Baroque style.

2 Rose Window
The Neo-Gothic Rose Window (left) over the Main Portal was recreated by Schulek after he found fragments of an earlier window during the 19th-century restoration of the church. The original had been bricked up in the Baroque period.

1 Béla Tower
Named after Béla IV, the stout Béla Tower retains a number of its original Gothic features, though the spire and turrets are all reconstructions. Note how the tower is the least embellished part of the church.

3 Altar
The early Gothic-style altar (right) features a replica of the holy Hungarian crown atop a statue of the Virgin Mary. A shrine to the Madonna, it was designed by Schulek and completed in 1893.

4 Loreto Chapel and Baroque Madonna
Legend has it that in 1686, the Madonna (right) appeared before the Turks defending Buda Castle, who saw it as a sign of imminent defeat. Habsburg troops took the castle that very night.

NEED TO KNOW
- MAP H2 ■ I, Szentháromság tér 2 ■ 06 489 07 16
- Guided tours available
- Dis. access ■ www.matyas-templom.hu

Open 9am–5pm Mon–Fri, 9am–1pm Sat, 1–5pm Sun. Adm Ft1,500. Closed for mass and events.

■ A programme giving times and dates of all upcoming classical concerts, held two or three evenings a week during the summer, is available at the main entrance to the church.

■ Ruszwurm, one of Budapest's most historic cafés (see p72), is just across the square and a short walk along Szentháromság utca.

5 Mary Portal
The finest example of Gothic stone carving in Hungary, this portal was rebuilt by Schulek in the 19th century, using surviving fragments of the original building.

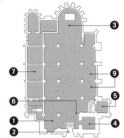

8 Sunday Mass
The church's two 1909 Rieger organs are the finest in Hungary, and Sunday Mass (at 10am) features the organs and the church's choir. A well-known centre of spiritual music, the church also plays host to more than 100 concerts a year.

KING MÁTYÁS

One of the greatest figures in Hungarian history, King Mátyás is often claimed by both Romanians and Serbs as being one of their own. What's certain is that Matei Corvin, as he is known in Romania, was born in Cluj-Napoca, in present-day Romania. He was the son of János Hunyadi, who in turn was the grandson of native Serbs. His family origins remain to this day one of the main causes of tension between Hungarian and Romanian historians *(see p14)*.

9 Stained-Glass Windows
Designed by Frigyes Schulek and painted by Károly Lotz, the three windows on the church's southern side depict the Virgin Mary's life, the family of Béla IV and the life of St Elizabeth of Árpádház, who was married at 13, widowed at 19 and died at 24.

6 Hidden Images of King Louis
Enter the church through the main portal and turn and look up to see images of King Louis the Great and his wife on the uppermost pillar beside the portal. They date from the 14th century.

7 Tomb of King Béla III and Anne de Châtillon
Schulek designed this elaborate tomb after the mortal remains of Béla III and his first wife were found during excavations at Székesfehérvár Cathedral in 1862.

10 Roof
The splendid multicoloured tiled roof **(below)** was added between 1950 and 1970. The original roof, a plain affair, burnt down after Soviet shelling during the siege of Buda in 1944–5.

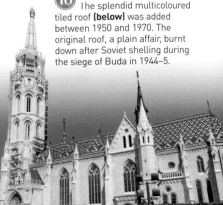

Hungarian State Opera

Nowhere in Budapest is the ancien regime as alive and well as at the Hungarian State Opera, architect Miklós Ybl's magnum opus. A Neo-Renaissance masterpiece built in 1884, when money was no object, its interior is a study in opulence and grandeur. A rival to any opera house in the world, its roll call of musical directors reads like a who's who of Central European music – Ferenc Erkel, Gustav Mahler, Otto Klemperer, among others.

4 Foyer Murals
Painted by Bertalan Székely and Mór Than, the foyer's sensational murals cover the entire ceiling and depict the nine Muses and other allegorical scenes.

1 Façade
The passage of time has been kind to Andrássy út, and the Hungarian State Opera is not as hemmed in as many of the city's other significant buildings. While in no way unique, the façade **(above)** of colonnades, balconies and loggias is impressive.

5 Main Stage
During the building of the Opera, the Vienna Ring Theatre was destroyed by fire. As a safety measure, an iron safety curtain and all-metal stage hydraulics plus a sprinkler system were installed, making the Hungarian Opera the most modern theatre in the world at that time.

2 Main Entrance
Stand under the Hungarian State Opera's sublime entrance with its muralled ceilings, and you will immediately wish you were part of 19th-century Budapest society, stepping out of a horse-drawn carriage to attend a premiere.

6 Statues of Liszt and Erkel
The busts of Hungary's two greatest composers – Franz Liszt and Ferenc Erkel – stand guard on either side of the entrance. Both were sculpted by Alajos Stróbl, who was responsible for much of the building's interior design.

3 Foyer
The foyer **(right)** is a wonderful riot of murals, columns, chandeliers and gilded vaulted ceilings. Ostentation to rival Vienna was the order of the day, and Ybl did not disappoint his patrons.

8 Main Staircase

A red carpet covers the marble stairs **(left)** beneath a huge chandelier in another of the Hungarian State Opera's classic set pieces. The gilded ceiling panels contain nine paintings (by Than) of the awakening and triumph of music.

BÁNK BÁN

Hungary's most famous opera, Bánk Bán, was written by Ferenc Erkel and premiered in 1861. The story begins with Otto, brother of Queen Gertrud, who plans to seduce the wife of a faithful Hungarian viceroy, Bánk. The knight Biberach tells Bánk of Otto's evil scheme, and Bánk decides to join in a rebellion against the court. Rarely performed today, it was made into a film by Csaba Káel in 2001.

10 Chandelier

Above the auditorium, a fine 2,722-kg (3-ton) Mainz chandelier **(left)** illuminates a magnificent fresco by Károly Lotz of the Greek gods on Olympus. The chimney located above it facilitates ventilation.

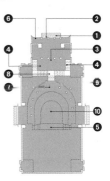

7 Royal Box

Ybl always insisted that the Royal Box was his finest achievement. With sculptures that symbolize the four operatic voices – soprano, alto, tenor and bass – it is in the centre of a circle of three-tiered boxes.

9 Museum

The museum houses memorabilia of famous performers who have graced this stage. Sándor Svéd, a renowned Hungarian baritone who performed at New York's Metropolitan for years, features prominently.

NEED TO KNOW

MAP M2 ■ VI, Andrássy út 22 ■ 06 814 71 00; Box office: 06 814 72 25; Guided tours: 06 332 81 97 ■ Dis. access ■ www.opera.hu ■ www.operavisit.hu

Guided tours: 3pm & 4pm daily; Ft2,900

■ View the façade, the main entrance and the foyer throughout the day, as the ticket office is open daily from 11am to 5pm. To see the rest of the building, join a guided tour.

■ The very best way to see the Opera House is by watching a show. Concert tickets are usually cheaper than in Western Europe, but for lower prices, visit the Erkel Theatre, at II. János Pál pápa tér 30 (06 332 61 50).

■ There is a great coffee bar, Balettcipő, nearby at 14 Hajós utca.

TOP 10 ★ Hungarian National Museum

Since its founding in 1802, this fascinating museum has been home to Hungary's finest collection of art, artifacts and documents relating to the country's troubled history. The building is a timeless piece of Neo-Classical architecture designed by Mihály Pollack, while the impressive interior has frescoes by Károly Lotz and Mór Than.

6 Processional Crucifix

This crucifix **(above)** from Szerecseny was made in the 12th century. A similar piece is in the St Stephen Museum in Székesfehérvár; the two are likely to have originated from the same workshop. In Hungary, many such crucifixes were found in churches destroyed during the Tatar invasion in 1241.

1 Monomachos Crown

The exquisitely crafted crown **(above)** is made of gold plaques that date from between 1042 and 1050. The gold leaf is decorated with allegories of the Great Virtues, which were popular in Byzantine art.

2 Coronation Mantle

This silk gown with the figures of Christ and the Apostles was given to a church in Székesfehérvár by St Stephen in 1031. It was later a coronation coat for Hungarian kings.

3 Funeral Crown

Found in Margaret Island's church in 1838, this golden crown dates from the 13th century and was worn by a female member of an Árpád family on her deathbed.

4 Electioneer-March in Front of the National Museum

As the title suggests, this pre-Secession painting by Franz Weiss shows the political campaigning of reformists and conservatives between 1847 and 1848, when, unlike most Western nations, Hungary was still characterized by feudalism.

7 Sabretache Plate, Galgóc

This plate is one of the finest examples of the palmette ornamental style of the Conquest period. In the shamanistic beliefs of the time, palmettes symbolized the Tree of Life.

5 Mozart's Clavichord

This travelling clavichord **(above)** was bought for the young Wolfgang Amadeus Mozart by his father, Leopold Mozart. It was used by the child prodigy to practise upon during their concert tours.

8 Diadem

Dating from the Hun period in the 5th century AD, the stunning gold diadem **(above)** is the most ancient of its kind. It was found in Csorna and is studded with 158 precious stones.

FERENC AND ISTVÁN SZÉCHENYI

The National Museum may not have existed at all without the vast collection of art and artifacts donated in 1802 by Count Ferenc Széchényi, who also established the National Library. His equally illustrious son, Count István Széchényi, is regarded as one of the greatest Hungarians. An aristocratic polymath, István wrote several treatises for the betterment of peasants, advocated land reform, dabbled in revolutionary politics and even paid for the country's first railway.

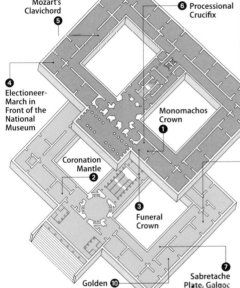

⑨ Red Engine

Mozart's Clavichord ⑤

⑥ Processional Crucifix

④ Electioneer-March in Front of the National Museum

Monomachos Crown ①

Coronation Mantle ②

⑧ Diadem

Key to Floorplan
- 1st floor
- 2nd floor

③ Funeral Crown

Golden Stag ⑩

Sabretache Plate, Galgoc ⑦

10 Golden Stag

An almost flawless hand-forged figure from the 6th century BC, the Golden Stag **(below)** was part of a Scythian prince's shield.

9 Red Engine

Painted by Sándor Bortnyik, this Cubist-style work is a fine example of activist art from the first quarter of the 20th century. Bold colours such as red and blue have been contrasted with white to highlight the sense of movement.

NEED TO KNOW

MAP M5 ■ VIII, Múzeum körút 14–16 ■ 06 338 21 22 ■ Dis. access ■ www.mnm.hu

Open 10am–6pm Tue– Sun. Adm Ft1,600; Ft800 for EU residents under 26 and over 62; free for over-70s

■ The Hungarian National Museum is set on three levels. The basement has a Roman mosaic, the first floor is home to exhibits from the 5th century BC to the Middle Ages, and the second floor houses exhibits dating from the 11th century to the present day.

■ There is a good café at the Múzeum Kávéház és Étterem (see p93), next to the National Museum.

TOP 10 ⭐ Great Synagogue

Europe's largest synagogue was built in a Byzantine-Moorish style to the designs of Viennese architect Ludwig Förster between 1854 and 1859. Accommodating more than 3,000 worshippers, it also features a museum packed with historical relics and Judaic devotional items, and a moving Holocaust Memorial.

Chandeliers ③
The two Spanish-style chandeliers **(right)** above the main aisle are similar to those at the Hungarian State Opera House: the design was common in concert halls throughout Europe at the time.

④ Organ Concerts
The original 5,000-pipe organ – installed in 1859 and played by Franz Liszt during the synagogue's dedication ceremony – was replaced with a mechanical organ in 1996. Concerts are held regularly throughout the summer.

① Twin Towers, Onion Domes
The Great Synagogue was the first in Europe to feature Oriental-inspired, Moorish towers **(above)**, complete with Byzantine onion domes. The towers are 43 m (140 ft) high.

② Upper Galleries
When built, the highly ornamented upper galleries **(above)** were designed for women who, according to tradition, had to worship separately. Today all worshippers sit downstairs.

⑤ Rose Windows
The rose window set into the façade above the main entrance is a reference to the architecture of Hungary's medieval churches.

⑥ Menorah Paving
A Menorah is depicted on the ground in front of the synagogue. Most visitors focus on the building, so it often goes unnoticed.

RAOUL WALLENBERG

Swedish diplomat Raoul Wallenberg is credited with saving as many as 100,000 Hungarian Jews during 1944–5, mainly by issuing them with Swedish travel documents. Wallenberg also negotiated directly with Major-General Gerhard Schmidthuber, head of the German forces in Hungary, to prevent the planned liquidation of the Budapest Ghetto early in January 1945. Days later however, after the Red Army had occupied Budapest, Wallenberg was arrested as a spy by the Soviet Union and taken to Moscow's Lubianka Prison. He is believed to have died of a heart attack there in 1947. He was declared Righteous Among the Nations by the Israeli government in 1996.

A memorial to Raoul Wallenberg stands on the corner of Szilágyi Erzsébet fasor and Nagyajtai utca (Map N1).

8 Jewish History Museum

Added in 1931, this museum (above) is home to a collection of historical Judaica from ancient Rome to the 20th century. In the rear courtyard there is a memorial to the 600,000 Hungarian Jews killed during the Holocaust. It is dedicated to Raoul Wallenberg.

9 The Ark

The Ark (above) contains a number of scrolls saved from other synagogues and hidden by Hungarian Catholic priests from the Nazis during World War II.

NEED TO KNOW

MAP D4 ▪ VII, Dohány utca 2 ▪ 06 462 04 77

Open Mar–Oct: 10am–6pm Sun–Thu, 10am–4pm Fri (1–28 Mar: to 3:30pm Fri); Nov–Feb: 10am–4pm Sun–Thu, 10am–2pm Fri. Hourly tours in several languages from 10:30am. Adm

▪ Tours of the Jewish Neighbourhood run six times a day (Sun–Fri).

▪ Kádár Étkezde, two blocks north, is a popular eatery offering Jewish-Hungarian cuisine (see p93).

7 Inscription Above the Main Entrance

Engraved in gold over the entrance is a verse in Hebrew from the book of Exodus: "And let them make me a sanctuary that I may dwell among them."

The Ten Commandments 10

Two stone tablets (above) sit atop the synagogue and are engraved in Hebrew with the Ten Commandments.

The Top 10
of Everything

**The thermal pool and Neo-Baroque
buildings of Széchenyi Baths**

Moments in History

1 AD 409: Huns Conquer Aquincum

Established in the area that now lies on the city's northern periphery, Aquincum *(see p101)* was an important town and military garrison in the Roman province of Pannonia. It was conquered by the Huns in AD 409, and subsequently ruled by the Goths, the Longobards and the Avars.

2 AD 896: Árpád Leads the Magyars into Pannonia

Prince Árpád led the nomadic Magyars – tribes which originated in the Urals and inhabited an area east of the River Tisza – into Pannonia in AD 896. He settled first on Csepel Island, in the middle of the Danube in southern Budapest, and later in Óbuda (meaning Ancient Buda in Hungarian).

Prince Árpád, leader of the Magyars

3 1000: Stephen I Crowned King

Stephen (István) was the first Magyar to accept Christianity and, for doing so, the pope crowned him king. He cemented the Árpád dynasty, which lasted a further 300 years.

4 1687: The Beginning of the Age of the Habsburgs

The Habsburgs became rulers of Hungary more by stealth than conquest. They completed their takeover in 1687, when the Hungarians gave up their right to elect their king, and ceded the crown to the Habsburg Empire. In one guise or another, they ruled Hungary until 1918.

5 1849: Chain Bridge Links Buda and Pest

The first permanent bridge over the Danube, the Chain Bridge was designed by Englishman William Tierney Clark, and built by a Scotsman, Adam Clark. Its completion in 1849 allowed the unification of Buda, Óbuda and Pest 24 years later.

6 1916: Charles IV Crowned Last King of Hungary

On the death of Emperor Franz József in 1916, Charles IV became king of Hungary. He abdicated in November 1918 and, despite attempting to regain the throne in 1919 after the defeat of Béla Kun's Communists, he was exiled to Madeira, Portugal, where he died in 1922.

7 1944: The Budapest Ghetto is Created

In 1944, the Nazis and their Hungarian allies, the Arrow Cross, herded over 70,000 Jews into the area around the Great Synagogue *(see pp36–7)*. Though well over 20,000 Jews died, 50,000 survived and were liberated by the Soviet army in February 1945.

Coronation of King Stephen I

⑧ 1956: The Hungarian Uprising

Following mass anti-Soviet demonstrations in October 1956, the Hungarian Communist Party's Central Committee elected the popular politican Imre Nagy as prime minister. On 4 November, however, just 18 days after he assumed office, the Soviet army invaded Hungary and crushed the new regime. Nagy was arrested and executed in 1958.

Crowds support the proclamation of the Republic of Hungary

⑨ 1989: The People's Republic Comes to a Peaceful End

Anticipating the changes that would eventually sweep through the whole of Eastern Europe, Communist authorities in Hungary sanctioned the creation of opposition political parties in February 1989. The People's Republic of Hungary became the Republic of Hungary in October, and in March 1990, free elections were held for the first time since 1947.

⑩ 2004: Hungary Joins the European Union

After ten years of negotiations, Hungary became a full member of the European Union on 1 June 2004. The occasion was marked with days of celebrations throughout the country, and was greeted positively by most of the population. Hungary had previously become a member of NATO in 1999.

TOP 10 GREAT HUNGARIANS

1 István Széchenyi (1790–1860)
Leader of modernization and economic reforms in the 19th century, given the epithet "The Greatest Hungarian".

2 Mihály Vörösmarty (1800–55)
19th-century poet and author of the epic *The Flight of Zalán*.

3 Ferenc (Franz) Liszt (1811–86)
Hungarian composer, regarded by many as the best pianist of all time.

4 Miklós Ybl (1814–91)
Architect whose work includes the peerless Hungarian State Opera *(see pp32–3)*.

5 Sándor Petőfi (1823–49)
Nationalist poet whose recital of his poem *Nemzeti Dal* (National Song) and the "12 pont" (12 points) on the steps of the National Museum in 1848 sparked a revolt *(see p34)*.

6 Béla Bartók (1881–1945)
One of the most important composers of the 20th century. He also collected and studied folk music.

7 László Bíró (1899–1985)
Eccentric journalist who invented the world's first ballpoint pen in 1939.

8 Attila József (1905–37)
Radical poet who wrote of love and despair.

9 Ferenc Puskás (1927–2006)
Footballer who led the great Hungarian team of the 1950s *(see p102)*.

10 István Szabó (b. 1938)
Film director who received an Oscar for his film *Mephisto* in 1981.

Ferenc (Franz) Liszt

🔟 Museums and Galleries

① Jewish Museum

MAP M4 ▪ VII, Dohány utca 2
▪ 06 342 89 49 ▪ Open Mar–Oct:
10am–6pm Sun–Thu, 10am–4:30pm
Fri; Nov–Feb: 10am–4pm Sun–Thu,
10am–2pm Fri ▪ Closed Jewish hols
▪ Adm ▪ www.milev.hu

Budapest's proud Jewish community
is based around the Great Synagogue
(see pp36–7), and the Jewish Museum
can be found in a wing to the left of the
Synagogue's main entrance. Established in 1931, it is home to thousands
of historic relics and devotional items.
There is also a room devoted to the
Holocaust and, in the courtyard, a
memorial to the 600,000 Hungarian
Jews who were killed by the Nazis.

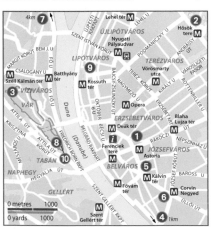

Artifacts in the Jewish Museum

② Museum of Fine Arts

Housed in a Neo-Classical
building, the Museum of Fine Arts
has a fine collection of pieces from
all artistic eras and genres. Raphael,
Toulouse-Lautrec, Picasso and
Goya all feature, and there are
also collections of ancient Egyptian
and Greek art. Closed for renovation
until 2018 *(see p95)*.

③ Museum of Military History

MAP A3 ▪ I, Tóth Árpád sétány 40
▪ 06 326 16 00 ▪ Open Apr–Sep:
10am–6pm Tue–Sun; Oct–Mar:
10am–4pm Tue–Sun ▪ Adm

Uniforms, flags, maps, weapons
and photographs document the
many battles that have been fought
in Budapest. The museum is
especially effective when it tells the
story of the 1956 National Uprising,
and of the many Hungarians who
subsequently lost their lives in the
repression that followed.

④ Ludwig Museum Budapest – Museum of Contemporary Art

MAP P2 ▪ IX, Palace of Arts,
Komor Marcell utca 1 ▪ 06 555 34
44 ▪ Open 10am–6pm Tue–Sun
▪ Closed Mon ▪ Adm
▪ www.ludwigmuseum.hu

If the dazzling splendour
of the Habsburg Empire
and the Secession
become too much for you,
head for this museum for
a refreshingly vibrant
display of modern
Hungarian art. More than
150 works dating from
1960 onwards document
the progression of
Hungarian artists as they
attempted to break out
of Socialist Realism.
There are also a number
of works by international
contemporary artists,
and changing exhibitions.

Hungarian National Museum interior

5 Hungarian National Museum

Founded on the personal collection of philanthropist Count Ferenc Széchenyi, the National Museum has been home to a stunning array of Hungarian artifacts since 1802, and the building is a masterpiece in its own right *(see pp34–5)*.

Exhibit at the Museum of Ethnography

6 Museum of Applied Arts

An outstanding museum displaying a wide range of decorative arts objects, including Oriental rugs, Zsolnay ceramics and Secessionist furniture. First opened in 1896 for Budapest's Millennium Celebrations, it is housed in a superb Secessionist building designed by Ödön Lechner *(see p90)*.

7 Vasarely Museum

MAP P1 ▪ III, Szentlélek tér 6 ▪ 06 388 75 51 ▪ Check website for opening hours ▪ www.vasarely.hu

Born Győző Vásárhelyi, Victor Vasarely was the founder of the Op Art movement in Paris in the 1930s. This museum, based in Zichy Palace *(see p51)*, is dedicated to his life and work but is closed for renovation until 2017.

Budapest History Museum

8 Hungarian National Gallery

Over 10,000 exhibits make the National Gallery's collection one of the greatest in the world. Spread across much of the Royal Palace, almost every significant Hungarian work of art from medieval times to the present day is displayed here *(see pp26–9)*.

9 Museum of Ethnography

Designed by Alajos Hauszmann, and built as the Ministry of Justice in 1893–6, this opulent building has been home to the Museum of Ethnography since 1947. The museum's collection includes costumes, toys and furnishings and paints a fascinating picture of everyday life at various points in Hungarian history *(see p80)*. The museum is due to move to new premises in late 2017.

10 Budapest History Museum

Set in the labyrinthine rooms of the castle, the layout of this museum can be tricky to navigate. Do persevere, as it gives fascinating insights into the history of the city. Its real strength is in covering the story of the castle itself, starting with the ruins of the medieval castle in the Palace basement *(see p69)*.

TOP 10 Places of Worship

NAGYME... ÚT / LIPÓTVÁROS / VÍZIVÁROS / VÁR

the stage for a number of seminal events, including the marriage of King Mátyás, and the coronations of Franz József I in 1867 and Charles IV in 1916 (see pp30–31).

3 Inner City Parish Church

Almost destroyed to make way for Elizabeth Bridge (see p48) when it was being rebuilt after World War II, the Inner City Parish Church was miraculously saved when the builders had a last-minute change of heart. The oldest building in Pest, dating from the 14th century, it was damaged by fire in 1723 and rebuilt by György Pauer in 1725–39. Don't miss the elegantly vaulted Gothic chapel (see p89).

1 St Stephen's Basilica

The grandest of Budapest's many spectacular churches is fittingly named after the country's first king, St Stephen. Built in the latter part of the 19th century, it dominates the city skyline and can be seen from most parts of Budapest (see pp16–17).

2 Mátyás Church

Mátyás Church has been bound up with Budapest history since the 13th century. It has been

4 Great Synagogue

Completed in 1859, this is the largest synagogue in Europe. Its design displays the desire of 19th-century Jews to assimilate into Hungarian society. The twin towers, for example, are clearly inspired by Christian church steeples. During World War II, the synagogue was used as a detention centre and also acted as the centre of the Budapest ghetto (see pp36–7).

Impressive nave of the Great Synagogue

Interior of the Cave Church

5 Cave Church

The remarkable Cave Church was built into Gellért Hill by Pauline monks following a pilgrimage to Lourdes. It was consecrated on Whit Sunday 1926. Bricked up during the Communist period, it reopened in August 1989 *(see p75)*.

6 St Anne's Church
MAP H1 ▪ I, Batthyány tér 7
▪ 06 201 63 64 ▪ Open 4:30–6pm daily

The twin-towered parish church of Víziváros is one of the most beautiful Baroque churches in Hungary. Built between 1740 and 1805, its highlights include the painted ceiling by Gergely Vogl, the high altar and the magnificent Baroque pulpit.

7 Serbian Church
MAP L5 ▪ V, Szerb utca 2–4
▪ Open 8am–7pm daily

Built by Serbian settlers in 1698, this Baroque church replaced an earlier one on the same site. The church's interior is arranged according to the Greek Orthodox tradition, as the Serbs follow the Orthodox liturgy. The iconostasis that surrounds the choir gallery and divides it from the sanctuary dates from 1850. It was carved by Serb sculptor Mihai Janic.

8 Lutheran Church
MAP L3 ▪ V, Deák tér 5 ▪ 06 483 21 50 ▪ Open 10am–6pm Tue–Sun

This striking church is characterized by its simplicity, in keeping with the design of most Protestant churches throughout Central Europe. Built between 1797 and 1808, it is not without charm. Superb acoustics make it a popular venue for classical and organ concerts.

9 Franciscan Church
MAP L4 ▪ V, Ferenciek tere 9
▪ 06 317 33 22 ▪ Open 5:30am–noon, 4–7:45pm daily

Founded in the 13th century, the Franciscan Church – like many in Budapest – was used as a mosque during the Turkish occupation in the 16th and 17th centuries. It was rebuilt by the Franciscan Order between 1727 and 1743, and their emblem remains visible in the main portal. Numerous sculptures of Franciscan saints decorate the church's façade.

Exterior of the Capuchin Church

10 Capuchin Church
MAP H2 ▪ I, Fő utca 32 ▪ 06 201 47 25 ▪ Open 10:15–11:45am Tue–Fri (also open by prior arrangement)

Just a short walk along Fő utca from St Anne's Church lies the charming Capuchin Church, a 19th-century replica of an earlier building. The first church on the site was founded in the 14th century, but was converted into a mosque during the Turkish occupation and almost completely destroyed in 1686. Of the few original features to remain is the doorway on the southern façade.

🔟 Baths and Swimming Pools

1 Gellért Hotel and Baths

Of all Budapest's many baths, this is perhaps the finest, so it is fortunate that it is open to non-residents every day of the year. The outdoor pools feature one of the world's first artificial wave machines (see pp20–21).

2 Lukács Baths

MAP B2 ▪ II, Frankel Leó út 25–9 ▪ 06 326 16 95 ▪ Open 6am–10pm daily ▪ Adm ▪ www.budapestspas.hu

Opened in 1894, the Neo-Classical Lukács Baths offer three outdoor swimming pools, plus three indoor thermal pools, along with Kneipp baths, fitness room, sauna and mud treatments.

3 Dagály Medicinal Baths and Strand

MAP P1 ▪ XIII, Népfürdő út 36 ▪ 06 452 45 56 ▪ Open 6am–7pm daily ▪ Adm

Some way from the city centre, the Dagály Strand is Budapest's largest pool complex, comprising 10 pools, including children's pools, plus a hydrotherapy and fitness centre. It will stay closed in 2017, when it hosts the World Aquatic Championships.

4 Széchenyi Baths

Set in a building designed by Győző Czigler in Városliget Park, the Széchenyi Baths offer a range of thermal water treatments. The complex has a number of outdoor and indoor pools (see p95).

Serene interior of Magnolia Day Spa

5 Magnolia Day Spa

MAP J2 ▪ V, Zoltán út 3 ▪ 06 269 06 10 ▪ Open 9am–9pm daily ▪ www.magnoliadayspa.hu

This spacious spa in the heart of Budapest offers more than 100 types of exclusive therapeutic massages, plus body and facial treatments, manicures and pedicures. They use only natural ingredients.

6 Hajós Alfréd National Swimming Pool

MAP B1 ▪ XIII, Margaret Island ▪ 06 450 42 00 ▪ Open 6am–4pm Mon–Fri, 6am–6pm Sat & Sun ▪ Adm

Designed by architect and sportsman Alfréd Hajós, who represented Hungary at the 1896 Olympic Games in swimming and football, the three sports pools (including an Olympic-size one) are still used by the Hungarian swimming team for training.

Outdoor pools at Széchenyi Baths

7 Palatinus Strand

MAP P1 ■ XIII, Margaret Island ■ 0620 212 98 73 ■ Undergoing renovation until mid-2017; check website for opening hours ■ Adm ■ http://en.palatinusstrand.hu

Budapest's most popular swimming complex has water slides, pools and hot springs, all set amidst the peace of Margaret Island.

8 Veli Bej Bath

MAP B2 ■ II, Árpád Fejedelem útja 7 ■ 06 438 86 42 ■ Open 6am– noon & 3–9pm daily ■ Adm; free for under-14s

Originally built in 1574, this Turkish bath has five thermal pools of varying temperatures, a Jacuzzi, two steam cabins, saunas, massage showers, a Kneipp bath, a swimming pool and a variety of wellness services.

The historic Rudas Baths

9 Rudas Baths

MAP K5 ■ I, Döbrentei tér 9 ■ 06 356 13 22 ■ Swimming pool: open 6am–10pm ■ Sauna: open 8am–10pm ■ Steam pools: open 6am–8pm for men Mon, Wed–Fri; women Tue; both Sat & Sun ■ Night bathing: 10pm–4am Fri & Sat ■ Adm ■ www.budapestspas.hu

The Rudas Baths, built by the Turks in the 16th century, are among the oldest in the city. There are six steam pools and a swimming pool.

10 Danubius Grand Hotel Margitsziget

Budapest's most exclusive baths are those at the opulent Danubius Grand Hotel Margitsziget *(see p23)*. Don't be surprised if you find a Hollywood star sharing the hot tub with you.

TOP 10 BATH TIPS

Relaxing shoulder massage

1 Etiquette
Most of the thermal baths are unisex. In single-sex baths and facilities swimming costumes are optional.

2 Payment
The price list, posted in Hungarian, German and English at the entrance to all the baths, usually runs to several pages. The entrance fee is charged according to the service you demand and is valid for a day. Last admission is 1 hour before closing time.

3 Towels
Bring your own towel, or hire one for a small fee and an additional deposit.

4 Bathrobes
In single-sex baths such as Rudas Baths, you will be handed a small sheet as a matter of course.

5 Lockers
Most baths have secure lockers where you can leave valuables for a small fee.

6 Water Temperature
All baths display the temperature of the water by the side of the pool.

7 Steam Rooms
Entrance to the steam room – where there is one – is usually included in the standard entrance fee.

8 Massage
Almost all baths and pools offer various forms of massage for an extra cost.

9 Wave Pools
Gellért, Dagály and Palatinus Strand all have artificial wave machines.

10 Family Bathing
Children are welcome in most of the city's baths, but the thermal baths are only for over-14s.

Hired towels

TOP 10 Danube Sights

The façade of the Hungarian Parliament, seen from the Danube

1 Hungarian Parliament

The city's number one sight looks better from the water or from the opposite bank of the Danube than from anywhere else. The splendour of its design – based on Britain's Houses of Parliament – is only enhanced by the river's soothing effect (see pp12–15).

2 River Cruises

MAP K4 ■ Mahart Passnave: V, Vigadó tér, Dock 5–6; 06 318 12 23, 06 484 40 13; www.mahartpassnave.hu

A number of companies run tours along the Danube in the summer months, departing from Vigadó tér. Mahart Passnave operates evening cruises – including drinks and dinner – to Vienna. There are also hydrofoil services to Vienna twice a week, running from the end of April to the end of September.

3 Elizabeth Bridge

MAP K5

Hailed the longest suspension bridge in the world when completed in 1903, Elizabeth Bridge (Erzsébet híd) had to be completely rebuilt after World War II, and did not reopen until 1963. Great care had to be taken on the Pest side to ensure that the Inner City Parish Church (see p89) was not damaged during rebuilding; indeed at one stage the church's continued existence was threatened, with the bridge-builders and the Communist authorities wanting to demolish it. A compromise was reached, however, and today the roadway passes just inches from the church's walls.

4 Shoes on the Danube

MAP J2

This moving memorial was created by sculptors Gyula Pauer and Can Togay in 2005, and comprises 60 pairs of iron shoes lined up at the edge of the Pest embankment, just south of the Hungarian Parliament building. The site had been used as a place of execution by fascist Arrow Cross militiamen, who shot hundreds of Jews here in 1944–5.

Shoes on the Danube

5 Margaret Island

Budapest's oasis and a great place to spend summer afternoons, Margaret Island was in fact three separate islands until they were joined together by ground-breaking embankment work in the latter part of the 19th century (see pp22–3).

6 Margaret Bridge
MAP B2

The gateway to Margaret Island (Margit híd) was built by a Frenchman, Ernest Gouin, from 1872 to 1876, and is distinguished by its unusual chevron shape. The approach road to the island, however, wasn't added until the 1890s.

7 Liberty Bridge
MAP L6

Legendary Hungarian *turul* birds sit atop the Modernist girders of Liberty Bridge (Szabadság híd). First built in 1894–99, it was destroyed by the Nazis during World War II – this is an exact replica of the original. It was earlier known as Emperor Franz József Bridge, but the Communists opted for a less imperial name.

8 Castle Hill Funicular
MAP H3 ▪ I, Buda Castle, Clark Ádám tér ▪ 06 201 91 28 ▪ Open 7:30am–10pm; closed 1st and 3rd Mon of every month & end of Mar–4 Apr ▪ Adm

Kids of all ages love to ride up and down the archaic funicular. The journey is short, the cabins tiny, but the views of the Danube below are superb. Also, on a chilly or rainy day, it beats walking up to the castle.

9 Embankment Walk
MAP B3, B4, C5 ▪ Columbus: V, Vigadó tér, Port 4; 06 266 90 13; Open noon–midnight daily ▪ Spoon Café & Lounge: V, Vigadó tér, Port 3; 06 411 09 33; Open noon–midnight daily

This walk extends along most of the Pest embankment, from Liberty Bridge to Margaret Island and beyond. Several boats moored on the various quays have cafés aboard, including Columbus and Spoon.

The Chain Bridge, linking Buda and Pest

10 Chain Bridge
MAP J3

Completed in 1849, the Chain Bridge (Széchenyi Lánchíd) was the first permanent crossing between Buda and Pest. On either side of the Bridge are two huge towers that support the mammoth chains from which the bridge takes its name. The towers are superbly lit at night, which makes the bridge one of the city's most photographed sights. In summer, the bridge closes at weekends to host a cultural festival.

🔟 Off the Beaten Track

1 Kiscelli Museum
MAP P1 ▪ III, Kiscelli utca 108
▪ 06 250 03 04 ▪ Open Apr–Oct:
10am–6pm Tue–Sun; Nov–Mar:
10am–4pm ▪ Adm

While the exhibitions at the Kiscelli Museum offer a fascinating look at the history of Budapest over the past three centuries, the real attraction here is the stunning building itself, an elegant 18th-century former monastery in a mix of architectural styles, perched on a wooded hill.

2 People's Park
Locals will always tell you that Városliget is for tourists, while real Budapesters head for Népliget. The name, after all, translates to mean People's Park. The park is home to the city's planetarium and, though it's hard to imagine today, its paths formed the circuit for the Hungarian Grand Prix in 1936 *(see p102)*.

Fresh produce stalls at Lehel Market

4 Lehel Market
MAP D2 ▪ XIII, Lehel ter
▪ Open daily

A bit of an eyesore from the outside, this is nevertheless the Budapest market to visit if you want a local shopping experience. Keep an eye open for old ladies *(nénis)* selling fresh produce direct from their own plots, as well as a huge range of delicious home-made cheeses.

5 Gül Baba Tomb
MAP B2 ▪ II, Mecset utca 14
▪ 06 250 03 04 ▪ Closed for
renovation until 2017 ▪ Adm

A 400-year-old dome covers the tomb of Gül Baba, a Muslim dervish who died in 1541, just after the fall of Buda. He was one of few Turks to be respected by the people of Hungary. Surrounded by a rose garden, the tomb is engraved with golden citations from the Koran.

6 Mikszáth Kálmán ter and Budapest VIII
MAP D5 ▪ XIII, Lehel tér

Even just a decade ago this square, along with much of the historic

The outdoor pool at Lukács Baths

3 Lukács Baths
Not as celebrated as some of the better known Budapest bath houses, the Lukács Baths offer a truly local experience. The ticketing system is complicated and you may need an English-speaking local to help you out, but it all adds to the impression that you are far from the tourist crowds here. Prices are much lower, too *(see p46)*.

Budapest VIII district, was something of a no-go area for tourists. However, private investment in its handsome yet long-neglected buildings has rejuvenated the whole area, and it now has an appealing bohemian vibe, with funky shops, chic galleries, and a buzzing nightclub scene. In summer, the square is a great place to people-watch, with locals and visitors enjoying the café terraces.

7 Fő tér, Óbuda
MAP P1

The focus of Fő tér, in the suburb of Óbuda, is the Zichy Palace, a must-see for those in the know, and home to museums dedicated to the avant-garde works of Vasarely (see p43) and Kassák (see p104). The Neo-Baroque Fő tér Palace opposite is perhaps even more impressive, while just north of the square on Laktanya utca is a group of statues, *Women with Umbrellas*, by contemporary sculptor Imre Varga.

8 Pálvölgy Caves

These caves are less well-known than the more accessible Szemlő-hegy Caves (see p101). The most spectacular sights at Pálvölgy can be reached only via steep ladders and by navigating tricky natural rock formations as part of a 3-hour tour with an experienced guide (see p103).

9 Páva Street Synagogue and the Holocaust Memorial Centre

Built in the 1920s, the Páva had fallen into disrepair after it was closed in 1941. Now a working synagogue, after restoration during 2002 and 2005, it hosts a Holocaust Memorial Centre. Its Wall of Victims bears the names of over 175,000 Hungarian Holocaust victims: more names are being added all the time.

Interior of Páva Street Synagogue

10 Aquincum

It's a pity that Aquincum – one of the largest Roman sites in central Europe – is not more popular with visitors to Budapest. Wandering its ancient streets is a joy, not least early in the morning, when you may have the place to yourself (see p101).

Ruined buildings of the ancient Roman city of Aquincum

🔟 Children's Attractions

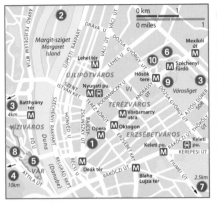

Model of a garage at Miniversum

③ Cogwheel Railway and Children's Railway

Cogwheel Railway: MAP N1–2; XII, Golfpálya út; 06 397 53 92; open 9am–4pm daily (last trains vary); adm; www.gyermekvasut. hu ■ Children's Railway: MAP N1–2; II, Városmajor station, Szilágyi Erzsébet fasor 16; 06 355 41 67; open 5am–11:45pm daily; adm; www.bkk.hu

Children aged 9 to 14 man a narrow-gauge railway that runs through the Buda Hills (see p101) from Széchenyi Hill to Hűvös Valley. The only adults on board are the engineers. To get to the train, take the cogwheel railway up from Városmajor. This track is 3,730 m (12,240 ft) long and climbs to 315 m (1,035 ft).

④ Csopa – Center of Scientific Wonders

MAP N3 ■ XXII, Nagytétényi út 37–43 ■ 06 814 80 50 ■ Open 10am–7pm daily ■ Adm ■ www.csopa.hu

Hungary's first hands-on science exhibition, Csopa offers a playful learning experience for all ages. Experience the world of physics here with over 100 live science shows and exhibits. There is also a family programme.

① Miniversum

MAP L2 ■ VI, Andrássy út 12 ■ Open 9am–7pm Sun–Thu (to 10pm Fri, Sat) ■ Adm ■ www.miniversum.hu

Get to know Budapest and Hungary in miniature. As well as delightfully reproduced city- and landscapes, there are scenes from everyday life around the country, plus an active rail network. In addition, games and treasure hunts provide a captivating hour or two for kids of all ages. The attention to detail is remarkable.

② Palatinus Strand

Margaret Island is home to Palatinus Strand, Budapest's most popular swimming pool and thermal bath complex. Slides and a variety of children's pools make it a popular choice for families (see p47).

⑤ Castle Hill Funicular

Children adore riding in the front cabin of the Castle Hill funicular. The journey takes just three minutes or so, but the views

Castle Hill Funicular

Acrobats at Capital Circus

of the Danube as you climb up to the castle are magnificent, and the two replica 1870 cars, Margit and Gellért, are charming (see p49).

⑥ Capital Circus

MAP E2 ■ XIV, Városliget (City Park), Állatkerti körút 12/a ■ 06 343 83 00 ■ Daily performances: 3pm Wed–Sat (also 7pm Sat) ■ Adm

This permanent circus, performing every Wednesday to Sunday, offers plenty of fun for all the family. The programme varies, but the focus is on remarkable feats of acrobatics, often from well known international acts. Light and water shows, high-wire acts and clowns often feature. In summer, the circus hosts the International Circus Festival. Shows are over two hours long, so may tire small children.

⑦ Planetarium

MAP P2 ■ X, Népliget ■ 06 263 18 11 ■ Open 9am–4pm Tue–Sun ■ Adm

Although small and by no means spectacular, Budapest's planetarium accurately charts the course of the planets and the stars, accompanied by a slightly dated pop and rock soundtrack. With shows throughout the day, it makes for a very good wet-weather option.

⑧ Labyrinth

MAP G2, G3 ■ I, Úri utca 9 ■ 06 212 02 07 ■ Open 10am–7pm daily ■ Adm ■ www.labirintus.eu

Make sure you don't lose your kids in this underground maze of tunnels and chambers. It is thought that the caves, which are around 15 m (49 ft) below ground level, were formed by hot springs about half a million years ago. They were a refuge for hunters and gatherers from around 10,000 BC, and even served as a bomb shelter during World War II. A special exhibition on the infamous prisoner Vlad Tepes, also known as Dracula, includes a torture chamber and mannequins of his victims.

⑨ Open-Air Skating Rink and Boating Lake

MAP E2 ■ Városliget (City Park), Budapest XIV ■ Boating Lake: Olof Palme sétány 5; 0620 261 52 09; open 10am–10pm; adm Ft1,200 (30 mins) ■ Skating Rink: open late Oct–early Mar; timings vary; adm; www.mujegpalya.hu

In winter, Városliget Lake turns into a superb skating rink, where people skate to classical music. During the summer, boats replace the skaters, as families row their craft around the lake. Skates and boats can both be hired at the jetty near the pavilion. There is also a visitors' centre.

Városliget Boating Lake

⑩ Budapest Zoo

Budapest's zoo is large, well funded and one of the best in the region. It has a large aquarium, an impressive aviary and a superb reptile house. The staff speak several languages and are good at educating children about the animals (see p97).

🔟 Restaurants

Interior of Onyx Restaurant

1 Onyx Restaurant
MAP K3 ▪ V, Vörösmarty tér 7–8 ▪ 0630 508 06 22 ▪ Open noon–2:30pm & 6:30–11pm Tue–Fri, 6:30–11pm Sat ▪ Dis. access ▪ www.onyxrestaurant.hu ▪ FFF

Connected to the legendary Gerbeaud Cukrászda (see p57), the Michelin-starred Onyx offers traditional gourmet cuisine in a welcoming environment (see p85).

Onyx seafood dish

2 Kacsa Vendéglő
MAP B3 ▪ I, Fő utca 75 ▪ 06 201 99 92 ▪ Open noon–midnight ▪ Dis. access ▪ www.kacsavendeglo.hu ▪ FFF

Kacsa means "duck" in Hungarian, so it's easy to guess what dominates the menu here. Duck is served in many inventive and delicious guises. There is a great deal more than duck on offer, however, and the wine list is simply superb.

3 Arany Kaviár
MAP G1 ▪ I, Ostrom utca 19 ▪ 06 201 67 37 ▪ Open noon–3pm, 6pm–midnight Tue–Sun ▪ FF

Just north of the Castle District, this gorgeous little restaurant serves an adventurous melange of local and Russian food. Every dish is a work of art, and can be accompanied by carefully chosen wines or one of a number of exclusive vodkas. The charming staff will help you make sense of the menu (see p73).

4 Costes
MAP M5 ▪ IX, Ráday utca 4 ▪ 06 219 06 96 ▪ Open 6:30pm–midnight Wed–Sun ▪ Dis. access ▪ www.costes.hu ▪ FFF

Local gourmets swear by this sleek, contemporary restaurant, which was the first in Budapest to receive a Michelin star (see p93).

5 Nobu
MAP K3 ▪ V, Kempinski Hotel Corvinus, Erzsébet tér 7–8 ▪ 06 429 42 42 ▪ Open noon–3pm & 6–11:45pm daily (lounge bar to 2am) ▪ Dis. access ▪ www.nobu restaurants.com ▪ FFF

The Budapest elite gather here to enjoy the sophisticated sushi bar or the private dining rooms.

6 Comme Chez Soi
MAP K4 ▪ V, Aranykéz utca 2 ▪ 06 318 39 43 ▪ Open noon–midnight Mon–Sat ▪ FFF

Despite the French name, this place serves fine Italian food, including some of the best seafood dishes in the city.

7 Baraka
MAP K3 ▪ Dorottya utca 6 ▪ 06 200 08 17 ▪ Open noon–3pm, 6–11pm daily ▪ Dis. access ▪ www.barakarestaurant.hu ▪ FFF

It is essential to book ahead for arguably Budapest's best restaurant. Head chef Norbert Biró dishes up creative cuisine and divine desserts. The service is also excellent.

The bar at Baraka

⑧ Búsuló Juhász Étterem

MAP B6 ■ XI, Kelenhegyi
út 58 ■ 06 209 16 49 ■ Open noon–
midnight daily ■ Dis. access
■ www.busulojuhasz.hu ■ FFF

The views from this traditional
restaurant on the slopes of Gellért
Hill are outstanding. However, the
food is average, and the Gypsy band
that shuttles from table to table can
either be a nuisance or a delight
depending on your mood *(see p79).*

Alabárdos Étterem

⑨ Alabárdos Étterem

MAP G2 ■ I, Országház utca 2
■ 06 356 08 51 ■ Open 7–11pm Mon–
Fri, noon–3pm & 7–11pm Sat ■ Dis.
access ■ www.alabardos.hu ■ FFF

This is about the only place to come
for Hungarian food as it used to be
cooked. From the goose-liver terrine
to the delicious chicken paprika with
curd strudel, everything on the menu
is authentic. Prices are high but the
food is worth every forint *(see p73).*

⑩ Kollázs

MAP K3 ■ V, Széchenyi István
tér 5–6 ■ 06 268 51 84 ■ 6:30am–1am
daily ■ Dis. access ■ FFF

The Gresham Palace Hotel *(see p83)*
has a long and illustrious history of
fine dining, and its latest flagship
restaurant is the best yet. First-class
food is served in a spectacular
Secession-style brasserie and bar.
In summer, diners can sit on a grand
terrace overlooking the Danube and
the Chain Bridge *(see p85).*

TOP 10 HUNGARIAN DISHES

Töltött paprika **(stuffed pepper)**

1 Libamáj Zsírjában
Goose liver, fried in its own fat,
is a Hungarian speciality and is
considered a great delicacy.

2 Kolbász
Sausages of all types. The classic
Hungarian sausage is usually
very spicy.

3 Bakonyi Sertésborda
Pork chop served in a creamy
mushroom sauce.

4 Bélszínszelet Budapest Módra
Classic Budapest beef and paprika
dish, though the beef needs to
be of very high quality to get the
best taste.

5 Marhapörkölt Tarhonyával
Traditional Hungarian beef goulash
in a hot, paprika sauce, often
accompanied by soft noodles.

6 Brassói Aprópecsenye
Pork stew, strongly seasoned
with garlic and paprika and
accompanied by fried potatoes.

7 Borjúbélszín Gundel Módra
Medallions of veal cooked in a rich
mushroom sauce.

8 Erdélyi Fatányéros
Popular Transylvanian mixed grill of
pork and beef, lavishly garnished with
pickles, peppers and chips. Presented
on a wooden platter, each portion is
intended to serve two people.

9 Töltött Paprika
Peppers stuffed with rice and mince
and served in a tomato sauce –
another Transylvanian favourite.

10 Halászlé
Hungarians do not cook much fish,
but this carp soup, seasoned with
paprika, is popular in winter.

TOP 10 Cafés, Pubs and Bars

1 Tóth Kocsma
MAP C2 ■ V, Falk Miksa utca 17
■ 06 302 64 42 ■ Open 3pm–midnight
Mon–Fri (from 5pm Sat)

Despite being close to the main sights, this place has the look and feel of a classic local Budapest pub. Well-priced drinks, including home-made cider, good bar food and pavement tables in nice weather. It's small, so be prepared to stand.

2 Szimpla Kert
MAP M3 ■ VII, Kazinczy utca 14
■ 06 352 41 98 ■ Open noon–3am daily

This is the biggest of the seventh district's so-called ruin pubs and one of the most renowned. There is an abundance of nooks and crannies inside the building, while the outdoor area offers ample seating, as well as movies during the summer. Szimpla also hosts a series of summertime concerts featuring jazz, rock, blues and more, all of which are free.

Hungarian wine bar Doblo

4 Doblo
MAP M3 ■ VII, Dob utca 20
■ 0620 398 88 63 ■ Open 2pm–2am daily (to 4am Thu–Sat)

There's exposed brickwork inside and out at this charming little bar, which serves one of the city's largest selections of Hungarian wines, almost all of which are available by the glass. Even the bar snacks menu has suggestions for the perfect accompanying wine.

5 Ötkert
MAP K2 ■ V, Zrínyi utca 4 ■ 06 330 86 52 ■ Open noon–midnight Sun–Tue, noon–4am Wed & Thu, noon–5am Fri & Sat

Budapest's ruin pubs are legendary, but this place gives the concept an upmarket makeover. The light meals and cocktails are great, but the service can be a touch surly.

Hip ruined-garden bar Szimpla Kert

3 Blue Bird Café
MAP M3 ■ VII, Dob utca 16 ■ 06 208 05 80 ■ Open 9am–10pm daily

Quirky design, award-winning coffee, big American-style breakfasts and huge slices of home-made cake make this just about the most popular café in town. It's also one of the most colourful: a riot of blue and gold. The Blue Bird also boasts a lovely interior courtyard, which makes for a blissfully cool escape from the summer heat.

6 Blue Tomato
MAP C2 ■ XIII, Pannónia utca 5 ■ 06 339 80 99 ■ Open noon–midnight Mon–Thu, noon–2am Fri & Sat, noon–11pm Sun

This is a big, spacious place set over two floors and selling Guinness on tap. As well as the pub and bar, there is also a high-end restaurant that serves international cuisine; try one of the steaks. The cellar houses the music zone, where DJs and bands will keep you entertained.

7 Boutiq'Bar
MAP L3 ▪ VI, Paulay Ede utca 5
▪ 0630 229 18 21 ▪ Open 6pm–late
Tue–Sat

Outside of the smart hotels, downtown Pest used to have a shortage of good cocktail bars, but that is no longer the case. The team of dedicated young mixologists here is adept at creating both classic and innovative cocktails. Prices are not cheap, but the quality of the drinks is superb, and the service impeccable.

Gerbeaud Cukrászda cakes

9 Gerbeaud Cukrászda (Café Gerbeaud)
MAP K3 ▪ V, Vörösmarty tér 7 ▪ 06 429 90 00 ▪ Open 9am–9pm daily

Possibly Budapest's most famous and elegant café, Gerbeaud is a real treat for coffee- and dessert-lovers, as well as for historians. It is worth stopping here simply to admire the brass cash register and the saloons complete with old chandeliers.

Stylish interior of Boutiq'Bar

8 Café Vian
MAP M2 ▪ VI, Liszt Ferenc tér 9
▪ 06 268 11 54 ▪ Open 9am–1am daily

Even with big-brand coffee houses opening all over Budapest, Café Vian continues to be busy both day and night. It is warm and inviting, contemporary yet traditional, and the coffee and food are fantastic.

10 New York Café és Étterem
MAP D4 ▪ VII, Erzsébet körút 9–11
▪ 06 322 38 49 ▪ Open 9am–midnight

This lavish coffee house and restaurant inside the New York Palace (now home to a hotel, see p114) has a fascinating history. Its richly frescoed ceilings and little gold chairs belie the fact that it was once a hangout for impoverished writers. The food is excellent, but portions can be small.

Opulent decor at the gleaming New York Café és Étterem

🔟 Shops and Markets

1 WestEnd City Center
MAP C2 ▪ VI, Váci út 1–3 ▪ 06 238 77 77 ▪ Open 10am–9pm Mon–Sat, 10am–6pm Sun ▪ Dis. access

This vast, three-level complex of more than 400 shops is next to Nyugati Railway Station. All your favourite brands and stores can be found here, though don't expect bargains, as prices are often higher than at home. Don't miss the rooftop garden. Some community events also take place here.

WestEnd City Center

2 Apponyi Márkabolt
MAP K3 ▪ V, József nádor tér 11 ▪ 06 317 26 22 ▪ Open 10am–6pm Mon–Fri, 10am–2pm Sat ▪ www.herend.com

As much a museum as it is a shop, Apponyi is an authorized retailer of Hungary's finest porcelain, known as Herend. The Herend factory, to the west of the city, has been making exquisite porcelain for generations. Most pieces at Apponyi command high prices, and everything is housed in large, priceless wooden cabinets beneath a splendid wooden ceiling.

3 Fashion Streets
MAP K3 ▪ Deák Ferenc utca ▪ MAP L2–L3 ▪ Andrássy út

Classy fashion stores and cafés dominate two of the city's most elegant shopping streets. Deák Ferenc utca (also called Fashion Street), which runs towards Váci utca, features brands such as Hugo Boss and Tommy Hilfiger. More glamorous options line the elegant Andrássy út (see p95), including Louis Vuitton and Gucci.

4 Gouba
MAP L3 ▪ Király utca 13 ▪ Open 10am–7pm ▪ www.gouba.hu

Between March and October, the Gouba (Gozsdu Bazaar) is held every Sunday in the Gozsdu Passage, offering diverse arts and crafts, gastronomic delights and entertainment.

5 Párizsi Nagyáruház
MAP M2 ▪ VI, Andrássy út 39 ▪ 06 484 80 00 ▪ Open 10am–10pm daily

The Paris Department Store is on Budapest's equivalent of Oxford Street or Fifth Avenue. This beautiful shopping centre specializes in books (with a generous selection of English-language titles), music, gifts and fine wine. There's also a delightful Art Nouveau café upstairs.

Central Market Hall

⑥ Central Market Hall
MAP M6 ■ V, Vámház körút 1–3 ■ 06 366 33 00 ■ Open 6am–5pm Mon, 6am–6pm Tue–Fri, 6am–3pm Sat ■ Dis. access

Budapest's main produce market is great for local delicacies. Impeccably clean, it has numerous stalls selling meat, salami, fruit and vegetables. The upper floor has several street food stalls, restaurants and souvenir shops.

⑦ Polgár Galéria
MAP M4 ■ V, Kossuth Lajos utca 3 ■ 06 318 69 54 ■ Open 10am–6pm Mon–Fri, 10am–1pm Sat ■ www.polgar-galeria.hu

A sensational art and antiques gallery, where you can purchase works by classical and contemporary Hungarian artists. You will also find rare antiques, including imperial Habsburg furniture. The gallery even looks after all onward shipping and related paperwork.

⑧ BÁV Jewellery (Rubin Ékszerbolt)
BÁV Jewellery: MAP L4; V, Párizsi utca 2; 06 318 62 17 ■ BÁV: MAP K3; V, Bécsi utca 1; 06 429 30 20 ■ Open (both shops) 10am–7pm Mon–Fri, 10am–2pm Sat ■ www.bav.hu

A collection of fine antique watches and jewellery from one of Hungary's best-known auction houses. There are several other BÁV shops across the city, with different specializations.

⑨ Memories of Hungary
MAP L3 ■ V, Hercegprímás út 8 ■ 06 780 58 44 ■ Open 10am–10pm daily ■ www.memoriesofhungary.hu

Located on the edge of St Stephen's Square, next door to the Basilica, Memories of Hungary sells a wide range of traditional products made by local craftsmen and artists. Pick up a souvenir from their wide range of fabrics, porcelain, ceramics, jewellery, toys, Rubik's Cubes and food items.

Memories of Hungary ceramics

⑩ Rózsavölgyi Szalon Arts & Café
MAP L4 ■ Szervita tér 5 ■ 06 318 35 00 ■ Open 10am–10pm Mon–Sat

Rózsavölgyi is a treasure-trove for musicians and lovers of music. Opened in 1912, this old store specializes in sheet music and records. Musical instruments are sold as well. It is also a venue for theatrical and musical performances and literary and fine arts events, which you can enjoy along with a cup of coffee or a light meal.

The Gouba art market

🔟 Budapest for Free

The Pest embankment

1 Pest Embankment

A walk along the Danube embankment from the Elizabeth Bridge to Parliament is an eye-opening trip through various eras of Hungarian history and architecture, all overseen by the Royal Palace on the opposite bank. Look out for street artists and musicians in summer, and pause to contemplate the moving Shoes on the Danube memorial (see pp48–9).

2 St Stephen's Basilica

You will need to pay a small fee to view the treasury or climb to the dome, but the main attractions of Budapest's largest church are free: the Main Altar, featuring a stunning marble statue of St Stephen (King István); the Gyula Benczúr portrait of István dedicating Hungary to the Virgin Mary; and the Holy Right Hand, believed to be the right forearm of István himself (see pp16–17).

3 Museums on National Holidays

Most of Hungary's state and municipal museums are free on national holidays (see p63). The National Museum (see pp34–5), the National Gallery (see pp26–9) and the Museum of Fine Arts (see p95) are the pick of the bunch. Note that the guided tour of Parliament (see pp12–15) is not free.

4 Walking Tours

Budding tour guides, and locals who simply want to share their knowledge of the city, offer a number of free, themed daily walking tours during spring and summer. The unofficial meeting point for these walks is the fountain in Vörösmarty tér: get here between 10am and 11am and you should have no problem finding one to join. Although free, your guide will appreciate a tip if you find the tour worthwhile.

5 Danube Carnival

Throughout June, the Danube Carnival takes over Vörösmarty tér, the Pest embankment and – on some weekends – the Chain Bridge. Most of the concerts, parades, street art and children's events held as part of the festival are free.

6 Gellért Hill

Gellért Hill (see p78) is surprisingly steep, and climbing up to the Citadel on the top offers something of a challenge to even the fittest. Make sure to stop to admire the Gellért Monument on the way up, before heading down the other side via the unique Cave Church (see p75).

7 Fishermen's Bastion

The defining view of Budapest is that offered from the turrets of the Fishermen's Bastion up on Castle Hill, from where you can pick out all of the city's major landmarks. Just make sure you get here early in the

Fishermen's Bastion

morning to get the best out of the place, as the crowds can be overwhelming later on (see p70).

8 Városliget

Central Budapest's largest park offers a wide range of free things to see and do, from admiring the Millennium Monument on Heroes' Square to enjoying a walk through its surprisingly densely forested paths. The park boasts a large number of flower beds around the central lake, a riot of colour in bloom (see pp94–7).

Vajdahunyad Castle, Városliget

9 Margaret Island

Elegant Margaret Island, a park since the 1860s, is where Budapest residents come to find a little peace. Walk from one length to the other, past the ruins of a 13th-century Dominican monastery, a UNESCO-protected water tower and through the lush Japanese Garden, all for free (see pp22–3).

10 Inner City Parish Church

While the Mátyás Church across the river gets all the attention and visitors (despite the steep entrance fee), most locals will tell you that the free Inner City Parish Church is even more impressive. Look out for remains of the original 15th-century frescoes, as well as the mihrab, a reminder of the Turkish occupation (see p89).

TOP 10 MONEY-SAVING TIPS

Hungarian wine

1 Buy a travelcard if using public transport. These are available for 1, 3 or 7 days and make travel much cheaper (see www.bkk.hu/en).

2 Most restaurants in the city centre – especially those close to office buildings – offer cheap set menu deals at lunchtime.

3 The yellow licensed taxis have the same, fixed fare. Make sure the price per kilometre is clearly displayed.

4 Look out for free concerts and street performers in Vörösmarty tér and along Váci utca.

5 Most hotels in Budapest tend to offer lower rates during the week.

6 Budapest's smarter hostels usually have private rooms with bathrooms, which are much cheaper than hotels.

7 Local Hungarian beer and wine is often cheaper than imported alcohol (and often tastes much better).

8 Do what local pensioners do and visit bath houses early in the morning to grab the lowest prices.

9 The Budapest Card offers free public transport and reduced price admission to a number of museums and other attractions (see www.budapest-card.com/en).

10 Budapest's main parks, Népliget and Városliget, are perfect for whiling away the hours – pack a picnic and relax.

Budapest taxi

🔟 Festivals and Events

Dancing and laser shows at Sziget Festival of pop and rock music

① Budapest Spring Festival
www.btf.hu

The Budapest Spring Festival runs for two weeks in April and features world-class performers. Outstanding opera, chamber and classical music, literature and theatre take over almost every performance art venue in the city.

② Budapest Dance Festival
www.budapesttancfesztival.hu

Paying tribute to the art of dance and usually held on 29 April (the Day of Dance), this festival introduces the season's productions, features foreign companies and honours the year's best Hungarian dance artists. The host institutes are the National Dance Theatre and Hungary's cultural hub, the Palace of Arts.

③ Budapest Summer Festival
www.szabadter.hu

The Budapest Summer Festival takes place every weekend from June until August. Both international and Hungarian theatre and music shows take place in the city's parks.

④ Hungarian Grand Prix
www.hungaroring.hu

The Hungaroring circuit is 19 km (12 miles) from Budapest. The city goes into Grand Prix mode at least a week before the race (usually the end of July). Tickets are expensive and best booked in advance.

⑤ Sziget Festival
www.sziget.hu

Central Europe's biggest pop and rock festival makes perfect use of Óbudai, an island in the middle of the Danube. The world's leading artistes perform over a week in mid-August. Most revellers stay on the island the whole week, sleeping in tents.

⑥ Festival of Folk Arts

Each year in August, Dísz tér in the Castle District comes alive for four days of arts and crafts. Skilled craftsmen from all over Hungary flock here to display and sell their wares. There are also performances of Hungarian folk music and dance. The highlight, however, is the craftsmen's parade that takes place on St Stephen's Day (20 August).

Parade at the Festival of Folk Arts

Jewish Summer Festival
www.zsidonyarifesztival.hu

This week-long celebration of Jewish culture is usually held at the end of August. It features music, dance, visual arts, comedy and cabaret. Full details are available at the Jewinform pavilion next to the Great Synagogue on Dohány utca (see pp36–7).

 Budapest Wine Festival
www.winefestival.hu

Every September, the area around Buda Castle is filled with Hungary's finest wine merchants and artisanal food producers, who display their latest offerings. There is also a parade and a charity wine auction.

Budapest Wine Festival

 Café Budapest Contemporary Arts Festival
www.cafebudapestfest.hu

"Art is communication; communication can best be learned through art". This message has driven the Budapest Autumn Festival for many years. One of Europe's leading celebrations of the contemporary arts, the festival makes a special effort to showcase the work of artists who have few opportunities open to them, and to stimulate communication among different genres.

 Christmas Fair
www.budapestinfo.hu

At the end of November, Vörösmarty Square turns into a festive market for Hungarian arts, crafts and food. At 5pm daily, a new window of the Advent calendar opens on the façade of Gerbeaud Cukrászda (see p57).

TOP 10 HOLIDAYS

1 Anniversary of 1848 Revolution (15 Mar)
Hungarians pay their respects to Sándor Petőfi by re-enacting his poem at the National Museum (see pp34–5).

2 Easter (Mar/Apr)
As a largely Catholic nation, Hungarians celebrate Easter quietly at home.

3 Whit Sunday and Monday (7th Sunday and the following Monday after Easter)
This national holiday celebrates the descent of the Holy Spirit.

4 Labour Day (1 May)
Once a Communist holiday marked with processions of workers, Labour Day is still observed as a national holiday.

5 St Stephen's Day (20 Aug)
Celebrates the coronation of St Stephen (István), Hungary's patron saint, with a firework display over the Danube.

6 Republic Day (23 Oct)
A double celebration commemorates the outbreak of the 1956 revolution and the 1989 proclamation of the Republic of Hungary.

7 All Saints' Day (1 Nov)
Celebrates saints who do not have their own holy days. The preceding day, people visit cemeteries to light candles in remembrance of their lost relatives.

8 Santa Claus Day (6 Dec)
This is when children hope to find small gifts left in their polished shoes by Santa Claus (Mikulás).

9 Christmas (24–26 Dec)
The city's famed Christmas gift market takes place throughout December.

10 New Year (31 Dec)
New Year's Eve is celebrated on the streets. Vörösmarty tér usually hosts pop concerts and firework displays.

Christmas Nativity scene

🔟 Day Trips from Budapest

① Visegrád
Bus from Árpád híd ▪ Castle: 0626 59 70 10; open May–Sep: 9am 5pm Tue–Sun ▪ Palace: open 9am–6pm Tue–Sun

The splendid ruins of a 13th-century castle are the focal point of Visegrád. The finest palace of its time, it stands atop a hill above the town. Visitors can also explore a 20th-century reconstruction of the palace.

Royal Palace at Gödöllő

② Gödöllő
HÉV from Örs Vezér tere ▪ Royal Palace: 0628 41 01 24; open Apr–Oct: 10am–6pm; Nov–Mar: 10am–4pm Mon–Fri; 10am–5pm Sat & Sun; www.kiralyikastely.hu

The 18th-century Royal Palace at Gödöllő hosts a museum and theatre. Open-air concerts and theatre are highlights, but the Baroque palace and museum – especially the Palace Chapel, Franz József's salon and the gardens – are also worth a look.

③ Fót
Bus from Árpád híd; train from Nyugati pu ▪ Palace: 0627 36 13 39

Fót is home to the Károlyi Palace, the birthplace of Hungary's first president, Mihály Károlyi. The Church of the Immaculate Conception, with its columned nave, is also worth a visit.

④ Kecskemét
Train from Nyugati pu ▪ Town Hall: 0676 51 22 63 ▪ Cifra Palace: 0676 48 07 76 ▪ www.kecskemet.hu

Ödön Lechner's town hall (1893–6), with pink tiles and minaret-like spires, is Kecskemét's biggest draw. Another fine building is the Secession-style Cifra Palace, built as a casino in 1902.

⑤ Ráckeve
Bus from Népliget ▪ Church: 0630 429 72 48

This town's highlight is its Orthodox church – the oldest in Hungary – which was built by Serb settlers in 1487. The interior walls are covered with well-preserved frescoes.

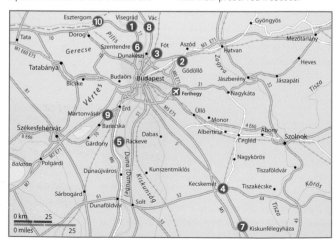

Colourful Fő tér, the main square in the riverside town of Szentendre

6 Szentendre
HÉV from Batthyány tér
■ Hungarian Open Air Museum: 0626
50 25 00; open Apr–1 Nov: 9am–5pm
Tue–Sun; 2 Nov–11 Dec: 10am–4pm
Sat & Sun; adm; www.skanzen.hu
■ Ferenczy Museum: 0626 31 02 44;
open 10am–6pm daily; adm;
www.szentendre.hu

With cobbled lanes, pastel-coloured
buildings and tall Orthodox church
spires, Szentendre is a picturesque
Hungarian town. Sights include
the Hungarian Open Air Museum,
which showcases country life from
the 18th century until World War I,
and the Ferenczy Museum's Margit
Kovács Ceramics Exhibition, which
displays the works of one of
Hungary's best ceramic artists.

7 Kiskunfélegyháza
Train from Nyugati pu ■ Park:
0676 48 26 11 ■ Tourist information:
0676 43 15 44 ; open 8am–4pm

Nationalist poet Sándor Petőfi (see
p41) spent a part of his childhood
in this town, and his house is now
a museum. East of town is the
Kiskunfélegyháza National Park.

8 Vác
Train from Nyugati pu ■ 0627
31 61 60 ■ www.tourinformvac.hu

Destroyed and rebuilt in the
17th century, this medieval town is
known for being the site of Hungary's
Arc de Triomph, built in 1764.

9 Martonvásár
Train from Déli pu ■ Brunswick
Palace: open 10am–noon, 2–5pm
(to 4pm winter) Tue–Sun ■ Park:
open summer: 8am–5pm; winter:
8am–4pm ■ www.martonvasar.hu

Brunswick Palace at Martonvásár
is one of the best-preserved stately
homes in Hungary. The present
19th-century building is a copy of an
earlier Baroque construction, built
in the late 18th century.

10 Esztergom
Bus from Árpád híd; train from
Nyugati pu ■ www.esztergom.hu

The capital city from the 10th to 13th
centuries, and the site of St Stephen's
baptism and coronation, Esztergom
has played an important role in
Hungarian history. The city's vast
cathedral is the seat of Roman
Catholicism in Hungary.

The cathedral at Esztergom

Budapest
Area by Area

The Danube, the Chain Bridge and
St Stephen's Basilica at dusk

TOP 10 The Castle District and North Buda

A UNESCO World Heritage Site, medieval Buda grew up around its 13th-century castle, which was erected on a hill to protect it from invaders. However, that wasn't enough to deter the Turks, who ravaged and then neglected Buda in the 16th century. It was the Habsburgs who finally restored the town in the 19th century, in glorious imperial style. North of the castle is Víziváros (Water Town), an area first inhabited by people too poor to live on Castle Hill. Today, it is one of the city's most exclusive residential districts.

AREA MAP OF THE CASTLE DISTRICT AND NORTH BUDA

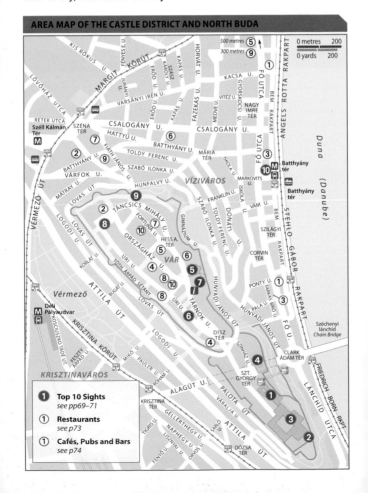

1	**Top 10 Sights** see pp69–71
1	**Restaurants** see p73
1	**Cafés, Pubs and Bars** see p74

① Royal Palace
MAP B4

Towering above Budapest, the Royal Palace, or castle, is an amalgamation of several buildings. Most of the present Habsburg Palace was built in the 18th century during the reign of Maria Theresa, but it was preceded by a palace and two castles. The first castle was built around 1255, but was rebuilt by Mátyás I in 1458. Following damage in World War II, the palace was renovated again, with some parts, such as the dome, being entirely rebuilt. It now houses several museums, including the Budapest History Museum and the Hungarian National Gallery.

② Budapest History Museum
MAP J4 ■ I, Wing E of the Royal Palace, Szent György tér 2 ■ 06 487 88 01 ■ Open Mar–Oct: 10am–6pm Tue–Sun; Nov–Feb: 10am–4pm Tue–Sun ■ Dis. access ■ www.btm.hu ■ Adm

Also known as the Castle Museum, this fascinating collection of artifacts and historical documents traces the city's and the castle's history via three distinct exhibitions. The basement houses a display on the castle during the Middle Ages that includes a recreation of a vaulted chapel from the earliest 1255 structure. Gothic sculptures and armour that were uncarthed while renovating the Royal Palace after World War II are also displayed. The ground floor has exhibits on the city's evolution from Roman times to the 17th century, while the first floor explores "Budapest in Modern Times".

③ Hungarian National Gallery

It would take weeks to view all the exhibits in the National Gallery, as there are thousands of works on display at any given time. From medieval altarpieces to striking Secession paintings, it's all here. The gallery shares its collection with the Museum of Fine Arts (see pp26–9).

Hungarian National Gallery

④ Sándor Palace
MAP H3 ■ I, Szent György tér 1–3 ■ Closed to the public

The official residence of the Hungarian president can only be admired from the outside, but the superb Neo-Classical motifs and bas-reliefs by Richárd Török, Miklós Melocco and Tamás Körössényi are worth spending time over. The Palace was commissioned in 1806 by Count Vincent Sándor, and designed by Mihály Pollack and Johann Aman. It was severely damaged in 1944, and was almost entirely rebuilt after World War II.

Budapest's Royal Palace

Interior of Mátyás Church

5 Mátyás Church

Standing on the site of a 13th-century structure, Mátyás Church was rebuilt and named after King Mátyás in 1470. Through most of the Middle Ages, Hungarians were not permitted in the church; only Germans could worship here. It has witnessed several significant events, from the marriage of Mátyás to the coronations of Franz József I and Charles IV. Béla III and his wife are also buried here. When the Turks came to power in the early 1500s, they converted Mátyás Church into a mosque. According to legend, in 1686 a statue of the Madonna appeared before the Turks while they were praying. They took this as a sign of defeat and surrendered the city of Buda to the Habsburgs. The church was also the scene of fierce fighting during World War II, and was not renovated until 1968 (see pp30–31).

6 Lords' Street
MAP G2 ▪ I, Úri utca

Baroque and Gothic façades give Lords' Street (Úri utca) its unique medieval character, though most of the houses were rebuilt from 1950 to 1960, after being destroyed during World War II. The street runs the full length of Castle Hill and its highlights include the Hölbling House at No. 31, with its sublime Gothic façade, the Telephony Museum at No. 49, and the bizarre but exceptional Labyrinth (see p53), whose entrance is at No. 9. The real highlight, however, is to walk from one end to the other.

7 Fishermen's Bastion
MAP H2 ▪ I, Halászbástya, Szentháromság tér ▪ Adm

From early morning until late at night, visitors bypass Mátyás Church and head for the Fishermen's Bastion, whose turrets offer the most picturesque views of Pest. It was built in Neo-Romanesque style by Frigyes Schulek as a monument to the Guild of Fishermen in 1895.

View from the Fishermen's Bastion

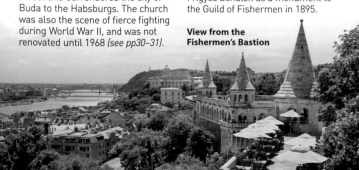

8 Church of
St Mary Magdalene

MAP G2 ▪ I, Kapisztrán tér 6

Built in the 13th century for the city's Hungarian citizens, who were forbidden from praying at Mátyás Church, this church now lies in ruins. All that remains is the tower and gate – the rest of the building was pulled down after World War II. Nevertheless, the site is enchanting, and the square in which it stands is unusually peaceful.

Vienna Gate Square

9 Vienna Gate Square

MAP G1 ▪ I, Bécsi kapu tér

The gate you see today is, in fact, a replica of the original structure, which once led from Buda towards Vienna. It was built in 1936 to celebrate the 250th anniversary of Buda's liberation from the Turks. Quintessential Gothic and Baroque houses line the sides of the square. The huge building on the square's left-hand side is the Hungarian National Archive, a Neo-Romanesque structure famous for its multicoloured roof.

10 Batthyány Square

MAP H1 ▪ I, Batthyány tér

In the heart of Víziváros, this square is named after Count Lajos Batthyány, the prime minister during the Hungarian Uprising of 1848–9. Though marred by traffic, the square is crammed with architectural wonders. The Hikisch House at No. 3 has bas-reliefs of the four seasons, and St Anne's Church (see p45) is a fine Baroque building. A monument to Ferenc Kölcsey, who wrote the words of the national anthem, overlooks the square.

A DAY IN THE CASTLE DISTRICT AND NORTH BUDA

> ▶ MORNING

There's no better way of getting up to the castle than by taking the **Funicular** (see p49) from Lánchíd utca. At the top, you can admire the stately **Sándor Palace** (see p69) from the outside, but you won't get past the smartly dressed guards unless you have business with the president. On the other side of the palace is the superb **Hungarian National Gallery** (see pp26–9). It would be easy to spend all day here, but with careful planning you should be able to see the highlights within an hour or so. Then stroll along the castle ramparts to **Lords' Street** (Úri utca), with its charming Baroque and Gothic buildings and end with a relaxing lunch at **Café Miró Vár** (see p72).

AFTERNOON

Head eastwards to the **Fishermen's Bastion** and enjoy fabulous views of the Danube and Pest on the opposite bank; don't forget your camera. Next door is the historic **Mátyás Church**. You can stock up on souvenirs at the shops on **Fortuna utca** – the Hilton Budapest hotel (see p114) has a superb souvenir shop – before following the road to the ruins of the **Church of St Mary Magdalene**. From the church, take the little Castle District bus back along Lords' Street to **Ruszwurm** (see p72) for a cake or strudel. If you are lucky, there will be a concert at Mátyás Church to enjoy as well.

See map on p68 ←

Cafés, Pubs and Bars

① Henri Belga Söröző
MAP H2 ▪ I, Bem rakpart 12 ▪ 06 201 50 82 ▪ Open noon–midnight

There are more than 20 types of Belgian beers to try at this pub, located next to a restaurant of the same name.

Oscar American Cocktail Bar

② Oscar American Cocktail Bar
MAP G1 ▪ I, Ostrom utca 14 ▪ 0620 214 25 25 ▪ Open 5pm–2am Mon–Wed, 5pm–4am Thu–Sat

Visit this sophisticated, cinema-themed bar to try a fantastic range of cocktails, either shaken or stirred.

③ Angelika
MAP H1 ▪ I, Batthyány tér 7 ▪ 06 225 16 53 ▪ Open Apr–Oct: 9am–midnight; Nov–Mar: 9am–11pm

This historic patisserie is in a former crypt of St Anne's Church (see p45). With its relaxed atmosphere and superb pastries, it is a popular spot.

④ Korona Kávéház
MAP H3 ▪ I, Dísz tér 16 ▪ 06 375 61 39 ▪ Open 10am–6pm

This excellent café is run by the same people that manage the Ruszwurm café.

⑤ Calgary Antik Drink Bar
MAP B2 ▪ II, Frankel Leó utca 24 ▪ 06 316 90 87 ▪ Open 4pm–4am

A cross between an antique shop, bar and club, the Calgary attracts crowds long after most places have closed.

⑥ Faust Wine Cellar
MAP G2 ▪ 1014, Hess András tér 1–3 ▪ 0620 398 88 63 ▪ Open 2–9pm Thu–Mon

Escape from the bustling city to this wine cellar in the Buda Castle District. There are wine and pálinka tastings daily, and wines can be purchased by the bottle.

⑦ Móri Borozó
MAP G1 ▪ I, Fiáth János utca 16 ▪ 06 214 92 16 ▪ Open 2–11pm daily

Wine straight from the barrel and drunk by the glass. There is usually a good stew cooking as well.

⑧ Café Miró Vár
MAP G2 ▪ I, Úri utca 30 ▪ 06 201 23 75 ▪ Open 9am–11pm

A colourful, popular place for coffee or a light meal. Service can be slow.

⑨ Café Gusto
MAP B2 ▪ I, Frankel Leó utca 12 ▪ 06 316 39 70 ▪ Open 10am–10pm Mon–Fri, 10am–4pm Sat

This charming café serves a good range of Italian coffees, along with generous salads and platters, and a selection of wines and spirits.

⑩ Ruszwurm
MAP G2 ▪ I, Szentháromság utca 7 ▪ 06 375 52 84 ▪ Open 10am–7pm daily

Ruszwurm has been serving cakes and pastries to a loyal clientele since 1824. The strudel is world-famous and the period furniture priceless.

Nostalgic interior of Ruszwurm

Restaurants

1 Kacsa Vendéglő

You'll need a string of superlatives to describe the duck dishes at this outstanding Buda restaurant. Service is ostentatious, with dishes whipped out from under tall silver domes *(see p54)*.

2 Baltazár

MAP G2 ▪ I, Országház utca 31 ▪ 06 300 70 50 ▪ Open 7:30am–11:45pm daily ▪ FF

Simple yet delicious food. Steaks, burgers, duck and chicken – all of which are locally sourced – at prices that are more than reasonable for the location. Grab a table on the cobbled street outside in summer.

3 Pavillon de Paris

MAP H2 ▪ I, Fő utca 20 ▪ 0620 509 34 30 ▪ Open noon–3pm & 6–10pm Tue–Sat ▪ FF

A lovely restaurant serving authentic French food, with seafood as the main speciality. It also has a great terrace and garden.

4 Fekete Holló

MAP G2 ▪ I, Országház utca 10 ▪ 06 356 23 67 ▪ Open 11am–midnight daily ▪ Dis. access ▪ FF

This restaurant has live folk music on most evenings. The game dishes come highly recommended.

5 Budavári Mátyás

MAP G2 ▪ I, Hess András tér 4 ▪ 06 375 61 75 ▪ Open 11am–11pm daily ▪ FFF

Locals flock to this beer bar to sit at one of the long tables and drink, eat and be merry. Join in and feast on their menu of simple but delicious gastronomical delights.

6 Csalogány 26

MAP A3 ▪ I, Csalogány utca 26 ▪ 06 201 78 92 ▪ Open noon–3pm & 7–10pm Tue–Sat ▪ FF

A modern restaurant serving simple Mediterranean food, mostly grilled on hot coals.

7 Hungarian Kitchen/21

MAP G2 ▪ I, Fortuna utca 21 ▪ 06 202 21 13 ▪ Open 11am–midnight ▪ FF

Here you'll enjoy a contemporary twist on Hungarian cuisine, with lighter ingredients. Dishes are cooked using fresh market produce.

8 Alabárdos Étterem

Sensational Hungarian cuisine cooked the traditional way. The army of chefs make a real effort to give each dish a unique touch. You'll be well rewarded for splurging on the pricey menu *(see p55)*.

Chic interior of Arany Kaviár

9 Arany Kaviár

The era of the Russian tsars is conjured up with caviar, blinis and champagne in truly opulent surroundings *(see p54)*.

10 Café Pierrot

MAP G2 ▪ I, Fortuna utca 14 ▪ 06 375 69 71 ▪ Open 11am–midnight daily ▪ FF

Founded as Budapest's first private café-restaurant in 1982, this wonderful little restaurant offers delicious food with great service.

See map on p68 ←

⓾ Gellért and Tabán

Ancient superstitions and medieval mysteries surround the areas of Gellért and Tabán. It is believed that Gellért Hill, which rises 140 m (460 ft) on the western bank of the Danube, was the scene of Bishop Gellért's death. In 1046, he was thrown from the top in a sealed barrel by enraged citizens, for attempting to convert them to Christianity. The hill was later the site of the Habsburgs' sinister Citadel, built to quell revolt and assert control. At the foot of the hill, the luxurious Gellért Hotel and Baths are a reminder of a gentler age. For centuries, Tabán was the city's most bohemian district, full of bars and gambling dens. More recently, urban planners have created parks and residential areas that now command some of the highest prices in the city.

Liberation Monument

AREA MAP OF GELLÉRT AND TABÁN

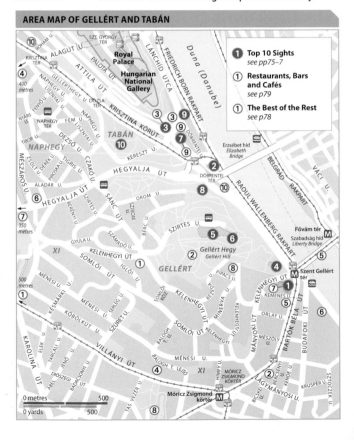

❶	**Top 10 Sights** see pp75-7
①	**Restaurants, Bars and Cafés** see p79
①	**The Best of the Rest** see p78

0 metres 500
0 yards 500

Gellért Baths' main pool

home was on the other side of the river, but it was removed by the Communists in 1947. It wasn't until 1986 that the statue was reinstated at its present site.

3 Golden Stag House
MAP J4 ■ I, Szarvas tér 1 ■ 06 375 64 51 ■ Open noon–11pm daily ■ www.aranyszarvas.hu

At the foot of Castle Hill lies the Golden Stag House, named for the superb bas-relief above its entrance depicting a golden stag pursued by two hunting hounds. This 19th-century house has long been home to the Aranyszarvas restaurant (see p79). Unsurprisingly, the eatery specializes in game dishes and features venison, hare, pheasant and wild duck.

4 Cave Church
MAP K6 ■ I, Szent Gellért rakpart 1 ■ 0620 775 24 72 ■ Open 8:30am–8pm daily

On Easter Monday 1951, the Hungarian secret police arrested the Pauline monks at the Cave Church, murdering the leader Ferenc Vezér and sentencing the others to long prison sentences. The church was then bricked up and forgotten until August 1989. This remarkable place of worship, which is hewn into the Gellért hillside, was founded by monks of the Pauline Order after they visited Lourdes, France, in 1926. The revived order once again presides over the church, which is closed to the public when services are in progress.

1 Gellért Baths

Built in 1918, these are the best known and most luxurious baths in all of Budapest. There is a sublime main pool, with balconies, columns and stained-glass windows, as well as more traditional thermal baths. In summer, the open-air swimming pools at the back are popular with chess-playing pensioners – many spend all day here. Although the baths are attached to the Gellért Hotel, their entrance is on the side street (see pp20–21).

2 Queen Elizabeth Monument
MAP J5

Although the wife of the Habsburg emperor, Franz József, was not Hungarian by birth, she adored her adopted subjects and made great efforts to soften Austrian attitudes towards Hungary. A number of streets, bridges and monuments throughout the nation are named after her. The monument dedicated to Elizabeth (Erzsébet) that overlooks the Danube from the Gellért embankment was designed by György Zala and erected in 1932. Its original

Interior of the Cave Church

Weaponry at the Citadel

5 Citadel
MAP J–K6

Built to intimidate Budapest's citizens after the failed Uprising of 1848–9, the Citadel was never actually used for its original purpose – that of preventing new revolts – as the Hungarians sought their independence by more peaceful means. Although the country was granted partial independence according to the Dual Monarchy agreement of 1867, Austrian forces occupied the Citadel until 1897. Today, the building itself, including the restaurant and the hotel on-site, are closed due to a long-lasting legal debate. Its look out points offer great views of the city.

6 Liberation Monument
MAP K6

One of the most visible landmarks in Budapest, this imposing cenotaph towers above the nearby Citadel. It was sculpted by Zsigmond Kisfaludi Stróbl and inaugurated in 1947, to commemorate the liberation of Budapest by Soviet forces. The inscription on the plinth once paid tribute to the Red Army, but was changed in 1992 and it now honours all those who "laid down their lives for

BISHOP GELLÉRT

During a pagan revolt in the 11th century, Bishop Gellért was thrown off Old Hill in a sealed barrel. To seek forgiveness from God, the citizens of Budapest decided to dedicate the hill to him a century later. Of Italian descent, the Bishop had, in fact, been invited to Hungary to help the newly baptized St Stephen (István) spread Christianity throughout the region. It was rumoured that Stephen's brother, Prince Vata, had a hand in the martyrdom. Today, the Bishop is worshipped as Budapest's patron saint.

Hungarian prosperity". Originally, a 6-m- (20-ft-) tall sculpture of a Soviet soldier equipped with a machine gun, with one of his fists clenched and the other holding a flag, stood at the foot of the monument, but this was later removed and relocated to Memento Park (see p102).

7 Tabán Parish Church
MAP J4 ■ I, Attila út 11
■ 06 375 54 91

This church is all that remains of Tabán's old district. Topped by a fine Neo-Baroque tower, it was built from 1728 to 1736 on the site of an earlier church that was converted into a mosque and later destroyed in the battle to overthrow the Ottoman Empire. Inside is a copy of the 12th-century carving, *Christ of Tabán*. The original is in the Budapest History Museum (see p69).

8 Gellért Monument
MAP J5

According to legend, the city's patron saint, Bishop Gellért was pushed off the hill that now bears his name for attempting to

Liberation Monument

convert Budapest's citizens to Christianity, including young Prince Imre, the son of Stephen I (István). Constructed in 1904, the monument to this Christian martyr is now looking a little the worse for wear, although it still retains its original majesty when viewed from afar. It is especially striking at night, when it is superbly lit. The statue and the enormous Neo-Classical colonnade that flanks it were designed by Gyula Jankovits and Imre Francsek.

View over Miklós Ybl Square

9 Miklós Ybl Square
MAP J4 ■ I, Ybl Miklós tér

Arguably Hungary's greatest architect, known for gems such as St Stephen's Basilica (see pp16–17), Miklós Ybl is honoured with a commemorative statue which stands in a square bearing his name. It was designed by Ede Mayer and erected here in 1894, three years after Ybl died.

10 Tabán
MAP H4

There is little left of Tabán's original character, as its narrow streets on the slopes of Gellért Hill were cleared in 1910 to make way for terraces, gardens and Secession buildings. It was one of the first inhabited areas of Buda – the Celtic Eravi settled it from 1000 BC. The Romans later built a watchtower here and, in the 16th century, the Turks built the Rácz Baths. In the 17th century, Tabán was home to Serb refugees, Greeks and Gypsies. Today, it is a popular venue for summer concerts, while in winter, the hillside is ideal for tobogganing.

A DAY IN GELLÉRT AND TABÁN

▶ MORNING

Start the day with a coffee and light breakfast on the corner terrace of the **Gellért Eszpresszó** (see p21) at the Gellért Hotel, then head around the corner to the **Gellért Baths** (see pp20–21). Try to resist the temptation to stay all day in the various baths and swimming pools; a few hours worth of pampering and a massage should be sufficient. Once refreshed, you'll be in fine form to tackle **Gellért Hill** (see p78) and climb up to the **Citadel**. After enjoying the views from its ramparts, break for lunch at **Búsuló Juhász Étterem** (see p79).

AFTERNOON

After lunch, descend southwards to the **Cave Church** (see p75), a bizarre place of worship hewn into the rock of Gellért Hill. From here, stroll down to Gellért Square and travel north along the embankment in the splendid tram No. 19 to **Miklós Ybl Square**. A short walk west leads you to the district of **Tabán**, where you'll be surrounded by Secession buildings. You can wander about the pretty terraces and gardens that replaced the earlier slum. Next, visit the **Tabán Parish Church** just off Attila út, one of the few surviving buildings from Tabán's old district. To the north is the fascinating **Semmelweis Museum of Medical History** (see p78). End the day by enjoying a classic Hungarian meal at the Aranyszarvas restaurant in the **Golden Stag House** (see p75).

See map on p74 ←

The Best of the Rest

1 Sas Hill Nature Reserve
MAP N2 ■ XI, Tájék utca 26
■ 0630 408 43 70 ■ Opening times
vary ■ Adm

A small reserve with a visitor centre giving information on the rare plants, insects and reptiles found here, including the Pannonian lizard.

2 Gellért Hill
MAP J6

The views from Gellért Hill, especially of the terraces below the Citadel, are among the best in the city.

3 Semmelweis Museum of Medical History
MAP J4 ■ I, Apród utca 1–3 ■ 06 375
35 33 ■ Open mid-Mar–Oct: 10:30am–
6pm Tue–Sun (to 4pm Nov–mid-Mar)
■ Adm ■ www.semmelweis.museum.hu

The house of the ground-breaking doctor Ignáz Semmelweis (1818–65) is now a museum. Exhibits include medicines from ancient Egypt to the present day.

4 Cistercian Church of St Imre
MAP B6 ■ XI, Villányi út 25
■ 06 466 58 86

This Neo-Baroque church was built in 1938. Inside are relics of St Imre, patron saint of the Cistercian Order.

5 Liberty Bridge
Built between 1894 and 1899 by János Feketeházy, this bridge was originally named after Emperor Franz József (see p49).

6 Technical University
MAP C6 ■ XI, Műegyetem
rakpart 3 ■ 06 463 11 11

Hungary's largest academic institution was built in 1904. Its alumni include Ernő Rubik, the inventor of the Rubik's Cube.

7 Budapest Congress Center
MAP A5 ■ XII, Jagelló út 1–3 ■ 06 372
54 00 ■ Dis. access ■ www.bcc.hu

Established in 1975, this arts complex houses the Novotel Budapest Hotel and conference rooms. It is best known for hosting concerts and major exhibitions.

8 Former Swedish Embassy
MAP K6 ■ XI, Minerva utca 3

This building was made famous by Swedish diplomat Raoul Wallenberg, who saved tens of thousands of Jews from Nazi death camps. A monument to him stands nearby.

9 Virág Benedek Building
MAP J4 ■ Apród utca 10
■ 06 201 70 93 ■ Open 2–6pm Wed,
Fri & Sat, 11am–6pm Sun ■ www.
museum.hu

This is the only remnant of the old Tabán area, which was detroyed by fire in 1810. It houses the Tabán History Museum.

10 Rudas Baths
The luxurious Rudas Baths (see p47), covered with a Turkish-style dome, are among the oldest in the city, dating from around 1550.

Liberty Bridge

Restaurants, Bars and Cafés

PRICE CATEGORIES

For a three-course meal for one, with half a bottle of wine (or equivalent meal), taxes and extra charges.

F under Ft5,000 **FF** Ft5,000–10,000
FFF over Ft10,000

1 Búsuló Juhász Étterem
The slopes of Gellért Hill provide a fabulous location for this traditional Hungarian restaurant. It specializes in game dishes and has a good wine list (see p55).

2 Marcello
MAP C6 ▪ XI, Bartók Béla út 40 ▪ 06 466 62 31 ▪ Open noon–11pm daily ▪ FF

A somewhat spartan pizzeria serving delicious thin and crispy pizzas at remarkably low prices. It's very popular, so you'll need a reservation.

3 Aranyszarvas
MAP J4 ▪ Szarvas tér 1 ▪ 06 375 64 51 ▪ Open noon–11pm daily ▪ FF

This friendly restaurant serves game specialities, as well as fish and poultry. The patio opens in summer and has a great view of the city.

4 Márványmenyasszony Étterem
MAP A4 ▪ XII, Márvány utca 6 ▪ 0630 625 85 59 ▪ Open noon–midnight daily ▪ Dis. access ▪ FF

Secluded and quiet – until the traditional folk band starts playing at 9pm – this is the perfect choice for an authentic Hungarian meal.

5 Szeged Étterem
MAP C6 ▪ XI, Bartók Béla út 1 ▪ 06 209 16 68 ▪ Open noon–11pm daily ▪ FF

A Hungarian restaurant next to the Gellért Hotel. The food is very good, and river-fish dishes are the speciality of the house.

6 János Étterem
MAP A5 ▪ XI, Hegyalja út 23 ▪ 06 202 34 14 ▪ Open nooon–midnight daily ▪ FFF

A surprisingly good eatery in a rather nondescript hotel. The menu is mainly made up of Hungarian classics.

Gellért Eszpresszó

7 Gellért Hotel
This hotel has three places to eat, each with its own terrace – the Eszpresszó, the Brasserie and the Panorama. The latter has an all-you-can-eat Sunday brunch (see pp20–21).

8 Hemingway Étterem
MAP P2 ▪ XI, Kosztolányi Dezső tér 2 ▪ 06 381 05 22 ▪ Open noon–midnight Mon–Fri, noon–4pm Sat ▪ Dis. access ▪

Escape the bustle of downtown with a mojito or a cigar on the terrace at this great seafood restaurant.

9 Asztalka
MAP J4 ▪ I, Döbrentei utca 15 ▪ 06 581 33 99 ▪ Open 3–6pm Wed–Fri, 1–6pm Sat, Sun ▪ F

This little café keeps short hours, but it is always busy. The range of cakes changes every day and there's a choice of gourmet coffees.

Cakes in Asztalka

10 Café Déryné
MAP G3 ▪ I, Krisztina tér 3 ▪ 06 225 14 07 ▪ Timings vary ▪ Dis. access ▪ FF

Popular with the locals, this family-friendly, French-style bistro is often packed for brunch at the weekend.

See map on p74

⅏ Around Parliament

Buda Castle and the Royal Palace may have the benefit
of their location on top of Castle Hill, but the city's
defining sight remains its splendid Parliament
building. The area around Parliament is redolent
with history and power, with large squares, wide
avenues and Secession architecture – remnants of
the once powerful Austro-Hungarian Empire. Several
of the city's most important buildings, including
St Stephen's Basilica and the outstanding Hungarian
State Opera, are located here. The area is also home
to some of Budapest's finest restaurants, as well
as its most exclusive shops and residences.

KOSSUTH

**Monument to Lajos Kossuth
in Kossuth Lajos Square**

AREA MAP AROUND PARLIAMENT

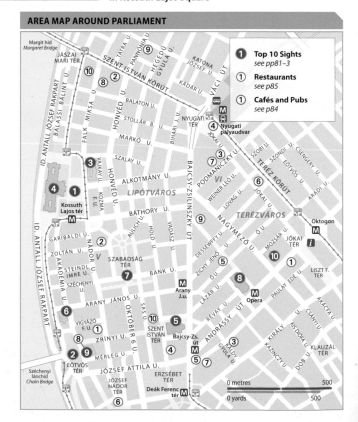

❶	Top 10 Sights see pp81–3
①	Restaurants see p85
①	Cafés and Pubs see p84

1 Kossuth Lajos Square
MAP K1 ▪ V, Kossuth Lajos tér

Still considered the best address in the city, Budapest's finest square is surrounded on all sides by splendid buildings. It was developed at the end of the 19th century, following the unification of Buda and Pest. The square is named after Lajos Kossuth, who led the 1848–9 Uprising against the Habsburgs and subsequently became a member of Hungary's first democratic government. He was exiled in 1849 after the Uprising was suppressed. A monument in front of the Parliament commemorates the Uprising. Opposite is another that pays tribute to Ferenc II Rákóczi, leader of the 1703 revolt against Austrian rule. A memorial to Imre Nagy, prime minister and leader of the 1956 revolt against the Soviet Union, also stands nearby.

2 Széchenyi István Square
MAP K3 ▪ V, Széchenyi István tér

This square has had various names: first called Unloading Square, it was renamed Franz József Square to mark the coronation. From 1947 to 2011 it was named after US president Franklin D Roosevelt and it is today named after the founder of the Academy of Sciences. The square features several fine hotels, including the Gresham Palace (see p83).

3 Museum of Ethnography
MAP K1 ▪ V, Kossuth Lajos tér 12 ▪ 06 473 24 00 ▪ Open 10am–6pm Tue–Sun ▪ Adm ▪ Dis. access (Szalay utca entrance) ▪ www.neprajz.hu

This splendid Neo-Classical building on Kossuth Lajos Square was designed by Alajos Hauszmann. It was home to the Ministry of Justice

Hungarian Parliament building

until 1947, after which it became the Museum of Ethnography. Like the Parliament, its grand exterior and richly ornamented interior reflect the majesty of the Austro-Hungarian Empire. The collection includes colourful displays of local costumes, toys, furnishings and wedding customs. The museum is expected to move to new premises in late 2017.

The Museum of Ethnography

4 Hungarian Parliament
Constructed in 1902 to house the National Assembly, Hungary's Parliament building remains the city's primary source of civic pride. It was designed by Imre Steindl, a professor at Budapest Technical University, who won an open competition held to find an architect for the building. Inspired by London's Houses of Parliament, this magnificent edifice is filled with paintings, frescoes and tapestries by renowned Hungarian artists. The interior can only be seen on one of the guided tours, which take place when Parliament is not in session (see pp12–15).

The impressive and colourful nave of St Stephen's Basilica

5 St Stephen's Basilica

Visible from all over the city, the dome of St Stephen's Basilica is exactly the same height as the Parliament's own dome. The church was built on the site of the Prank Theatre, where bears and wolves tore each other to shreds in front of crowds in the 18th century. Today, it is one of the city's most sacred sites, as it houses the mummified right hand of St Stephen (István) *(see pp16–17)*.

6 Academy of Sciences

MAP K2 ■ V, Széchenyi István tér 9 ■ 06 411 64 89 ■ Open 11am–4pm Mon & Fri

Inaugurated in 1864, the Academy of Sciences is a classic piece of Neo-Renaissance architecture designed by Friedrich Stüler. The statues on the façade, including those of Isaac Newton and René Descartes, are by Miklós Izsó and Emil Wolff, while the interior features more statues by Izsó.

7 Liberty Square

MAP K2 ■ V, Szabadság tér

Laid out in 1886 on the site of the barracks that housed the Austrian army, Liberty Square has long been synonymous with Hungary's freedom struggle. The first prime minister of independent Hungary, Count Lajos Batthyány, was executed in the barracks on 6 Oct 1849. The square was also the site of the 1956 protests against the Soviet Union. Today, an eternal flame at the corner of Aulich utca and Hold utca pays tribute to Batthyány, while the statue on the northern side honours Soviet troops who liberated the city in 1944–5.

8 Hungarian State Opera

This stunning building is one of Europe's concert halls, and the best way to see it is by attending a performance. World-class operas and ballets are performed almost every evening, and tickets are very reasonably priced *(see pp32–3)*.

Hungarian State Opera auditorium

SIR THOMAS GRESHAM

Although one of the city's finest buildings bears his name, Sir Thomas Gresham (below) never set foot in Budapest. Gresham Palace was commissioned over 300 years after his death by the insurance company he had established. The principal figure in the founding of the London Royal Exchange, Gresham is best remembered for the maxim he made famous: "bad money drives out good".

9 Gresham Palace

MAP K3 ▪ V, Széchenyi István tér 5–7 ▪ 06 268 60 00 ▪ Open 24 hours daily ▪ Dis. access ▪ www.fourseasons.com/budapest

Designed by Zsigmond Quittner and the brothers József and László Vágó in 1907, Gresham Palace enjoys one of Budapest's best locations opposite the Chain Bridge. It is an imposing edifice with several Secessionist features, from stained-glass windows (including one featuring a portrait of the patriot Lajos Kossuth), to its high atrium and chandelier. Today it houses a Four Seasons hotel (see p116).

10 Operetta Theatre

MAP M2 ▪ VI, Nagymező utca 17 ▪ 06 472 20 30 ▪ by appointment only ▪ www.operettszinhaz.hu

Operettas (one-act or light operas) have been performed here since 1898, when the building opened as the Orfeum Theatre. Designed by Viennese architects Fellner and Helmer, it was modified and renamed the Operetta Theatre in 1923, as it provided a home for the thriving operetta scene. It was further renovated in 1999–2001, but the interior remained faithful to the original design.

A DAY AROUND PARLIAMENT

▶ MORNING

Start with a sandwich or one of the excellent sweets at the **Szamos Today** café (Kossuth Lajos tér 10; 06 269 02 16; open 7:30am–7pm daily) next to the Kossuth Lajos tér metro station. Follow this with a leisurely stroll, crossing **Kossuth Lajos Square** (see p81) to the sensational **Hungarian Parliament** (see pp12–15). Here you can join one of several guided tours, which are the only way to see the building. After this, walk along the scenic Danube embankment to **Széchenyi István Square** at the head of the **Chain Bridge** (see p49). You can end with a light lunch on the terrace of the **Four Seasons Hotel Gresham Palace**.

AFTERNOON

Walk along **Zrinyi utca**, one of Budapest's foremost residential streets, famous for its smart Secessionist-style apartment buildings, to the magnificent **St Stephen's Basilica** (see pp16–17) on St Stephen's Square. Climb the steps to the top of the church's dome for splendid views of the city. Then head to the **Hungarian State Opera** (see pp32–3), timing your arrival to coincide with one of the daily guided tours at 3pm and 4pm. Eat an early dinner at the popular **Klassz** (see p85) and then prepare for a night at the Opera (make sure you reserve tickets in advance). Afterwards, a drink at nearby **Boutiq'Bar** (see p84) will round off a splendid day.

See map on p80 ⬅

Cafés and Pubs

1 Ötkert

This self-consciously hip designer bar is modelled on the ruined-garden bars typical of the seventh district *(see p56)*.

Courtyard at trendy Ötkert

2 Európa Kávéház

MAP C2 ■ Szent István Krt 7–9
■ 06 312 23 62 ■ Open 7am–8pm daily

Classic café serving pastries, cakes and perhaps the city's best selection of hot chocolate: there are at least eight different kinds.

3 Desszert.Neked

MAP M2 ■ Paulay Ede utca 17
■ 0620 253 15 19 ■ Open 11am–9pm Mon–Fri, 10am–9pm Sat, Sun

This café offers new-wave French and Hungarian pastries. Many of the best-known local cakes get a modern twist.

4 The Box Donut

MAP L1 ■ Teréz körút 62
■ Open 7:42am–8:08pm Mon–Sat, 9:42am–8:08 pm Sun

This place shows you how to straighten a circle: they serve square-shaped handmade doughnuts in 25 flavours, plus sandwiches and coffee.

5 Vakegér Tőzsdekocsma

MAP M2 ■ VI, Paulay Ede utca 2
■ 06 266 02 70 ■ Open 6pm–2am daily

At the "Blind Mouse Stock Exchange Pub", prices rise and fall depending on how often a particular drink is bought. Watch out for a market crash, when all prices plummet!

6 La Delizia

MAP M1 ■ Jókai utca 13
■ Open 10am–8pm Mon–Sat

This small shop and café sells a wide range of handmade cookies and healthy, sugar-, lactose- and gluten-free desserts.

7 Boutiq'Bar

Boutiq'Bar gets very busy after 9pm. The cocktails are excellent and the bartenders polished *(see p57)*.

8 Tóth Kocsma

This is very much a quintessential Budapest pub. Places like this used to be ubiquitous, but most have been squeezed out of the city centre by trendier venues. A must if you want a pint or a *palinka* with the locals. Try the elderflower cider *(see p56)*.

9 Blue Tomato

The interesting menu of modern Hungarian dishes is the main draw at this pub. A cosy ambience is created with vintage Americana posters on the wooden walls *(see p56)*.

10 Tokaji Borozó

MAP C3 ■ V, Falk Miksa utca 32 ■ 06 269 31 43 ■ Open noon–9pm Mon–Fri

This Hungarian wine bar is dedicated to the famed sweet dessert wines that are sold under the Tokaji name. Most patrons tend to enjoy a glass standing at the bar in traditional style.

Restaurants

PRICE CATEGORIES
For a three-course meal for one, with half a bottle of wine (or equivalent meal), taxes and extra charges.

F under Ft5,000   FF Ft5,000–10,000
FFF over Ft10,000

1 Klassz
MAP M2 ▪ VI, Andrássy út 41 ▪ Open 11:30am–11pm daily ▪ FF

A modern bistro offering international dishes, made using local ingredients, and excellent wines. No reservations.

2 Iguana
MAP K2 ▪ V, Zoltán utca 16 ▪ 06 331 43 52 ▪ Open 11:30–12:30am daily ▪ Dis. access ▪ FF

Great Tex-Mex fare in a lively setting. Fajitas, tortillas and burritos come in large portions at reasonable prices.

3 Ape Regina Restaurant & Bar
MAP L1 ▪ Podmaniczky utca 18 ▪ 0630 779 75 45 ▪ Open noon–midnight daily ▪ FF

Ape Regina is an all-you-can-eat Italian restaurant. Some drinks are also included in the fixed price.

4 Stradivari Restaurant
MAP L3 ▪ Hercegprímás utca 5 ▪ 0630 438 88 24 ▪ FFF

This stylish restaurant in the Aria hotel offers bistro-style dining. Afterwards, enjoy drinks at the High Note SkyBar on the top floor while taking in the splendid city panorama.

5 Imázs Restaurant
MAP L2 ▪ 1065, Hajós utca 16–18 ▪ 06 269 32 63 ▪ Open daily ▪ Dis. access ▪ FF

Located in the heart of Budapest, this restaurant serves great Thai and Japanese cuisine.

6 Onyx Restaurant
Szabina Szullo, the executive chef at this restaurant, is the first Hungarian chef to win a Michelin star. Enjoy the haute cuisine without spending a fortune by selecting one of the set menus (see p54).

7 Sir Lancelot
MAP C3 ▪ VI, Podmaniczky utca 14 ▪ 06 302 44 56 ▪ Open noon–1am ▪ FF

This themed restaurant serves huge portions of medieval dishes, from marrow bones and pork knuckles to whole geese and chickens.

8 Kollázs
In the gorgeous Gresham Palace (see p83) you can dine on clever, inventive dishes or enjoy the simpler delights. Dishes include snacks such as goose crackling and beef confit burgers, and refined mains like salt-baked sea bass (see p55).

Elegant interior of Kollázs

9 Marquis de Salade
MAP L2 ▪ VI, Hajós utca 43 ▪ 06 302 40 86 ▪ Open noon–1am daily ▪ FF

This popular bistro serves a range of dishes from the countries of the former Soviet Union, especially Azerbaijan, and includes a good vegetarian selection.

10 Café Kör
MAP L3 ▪ V, Sas utca 17 ▪ 06 311 00 53 ▪ Open 10am–10pm Mon–Sat ▪ FF

This eatery is legendary among the expat community, who flock here for light meals, good drinks and great atmosphere. Note that credit cards are not accepted.

See map on p80

TOP 10 Central Pest

Most visitors to Budapest head straight for this area, known as Belváros or the Inner City. It is the city's commercial hub, and is filled with fine buildings, shops and cafés. The area lay in ruins at the end of the 17th century, and was only redeveloped in the 19th century when many of Pest's most important buildings were built, including the Hungarian National Museum. Today, many of the streets and squares are entirely pedestrianized, making it an ideal place for walking, shopping and dining outdoors. In fact, during the summer, the southern end of Váci utca becomes a never-ending melee of cafés and pubs, with revellers drinking on the pavements from dawn to dusk.

Artifact in the Hungarian National Museum

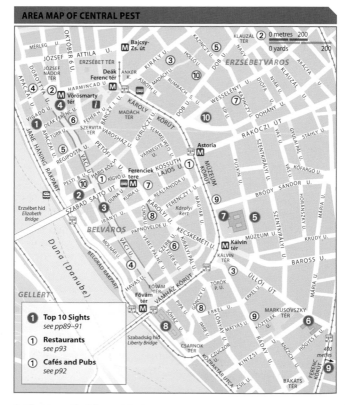

AREA MAP OF CENTRAL PEST

1 **Top 10 Sights**
see pp89–91

1 **Restaurants**
see p93

1 **Cafés and Pubs**
see p92

Previous pages The Fishermen's Bastion

1 Vigadó Square
MAP K4 ■ V, Vigadó tér

Facing the Danube, Vigadó Square is one of Budapest's quietest spots. It is dominated by the Vigadó Concert Hall, under whose sublime colonnades visitors seek shade during hot summer afternoons. Built between 1859 and 1864 and designed by Frigyes Feszl, it replaced an earlier hall that was destroyed during the 1848–9 Uprising. The façade is a wonder of arched windows, statues and busts. In the centre is a Hungarian coat of arms. Badly damaged in World War II, restoration efforts have faithfully returned the building to its former glory. Facing the Hall is the Modernist Budapest Marriott Hotel *(see p116)*, built in 1969. The jetties on the square's embankment are the departure point for Danube river cruises.

2 Inner City Parish Church
**MAP K4 ■ V, Március 15 tér 2
■ 06 318 31 08 ■ Open 9am–7pm daily**

Pest's oldest church has a long and troubled history. The original Roman-style structure was decimated by the Tartars, and its 14th-century replacement was converted into a mosque by the Turks. It was nearly destroyed again after World War II, when builders wanted to

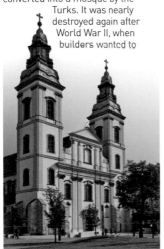

Façade of the Inner City Parish Church

demolish it to make way for the Elizabeth Bridge. Luckily, it was saved at the last minute, but the proximity of the approach road to its walls shows what a close call it was.

Pedestrianized Váci utca

3 Váci utca
MAP K4 ■ V, Vigadó tér

One of Pest's oldest streets, Váci utca originally led to the town of Vác *(see p65)*. It has long been synonymous with traders and swindlers, who clustered around Vác Gate at Váci utca 3. As Pest prospered, so did the street, and it soon became a favourite among Budapest's wealthy citizens. The goods stores gave way to exclusive boutiques, and today it is one of the city's most popular shopping venues. The northern half is dominated by retail outlets and department stores. The pedestrianized southern end of Váci utca is home to some of the area's best cafés and clubs *(see pp18–19)*.

4 Vörösmarty Square
MAP K3 ■ V, Vörösmarty tér

This splendid pedestrian plaza is named after the poet Mihály Vörösmarty, whose statue stands at its centre. Designed by Ede Telcs and built in Carrara marble, the statue rallies the nation in the poet's own words: "Your homeland, Hungary, serve unwaveringly". The square's northern side is dominated by Gerbeaud Cukrászda *(see pp18 & 57)*, Hungary's most famous coffee house. It is also worth visiting the quaint metro station.

JEWISH QUARTER

Budapest's Jewish quarter is based immediately north of Károly körút. The community thrived until 1941, when anti-Semitic laws were passed by the government of Admiral Horthy. In 1944 much of the area was a ghetto, and thousands were deported to death camps. Today the community is once again growing, with synagogues, shops and kosher restaurants.

5 Mihály Pollack Square
MAP D5 ■ V, Pollack Mihály tér

Named after the architect of several Neo-Classical buildings including the National Museum, this square is famous for its three palaces, built for Hungary's wealthiest aristocrats – Count Károlyi at No. 6, Prince Eszterházy at No. 8 and Prince Festetics at No. 10. The superb façades of the palaces (of which only the Festetics Palace is open to the public), make the square one of the most picturesque in the city.

6 Museum of Applied Arts
MAP D5 ■ IX, Üllői út 33–7
■ 06 456 51 07 ■ Open 10am–6pm
Tue–Sun ■ Dis. access ■ Adm
■ www.imm.hu

The opening of this museum was the finale of the city's 1896 Millennium celebrations. Created to house the Hungarian State's sizeable collection of art, the exquisite Secessionist building

Dome of the Museum of Applied Arts

was designed by Ödön Lechner and Gyula Pártos. Its distinctly Eastern style is seen in the green domes and the glass-roofed courtyard. It features fine arts, crafts and traditional costumes.

Hungarian National Museum

7 Hungarian National Museum

The National Museum was founded in 1802, and owes its existence to Count Ferenc Széchényi (see p35), who donated his collections of books and art to the nation. The building was designed by Mihály Pollack and completed in 1845. In 1848, it was the scene of a historic event, when Sándor Petőfi recited his poem *Nemzeti Dal* (National Song) from the steps, thus igniting the Uprising of 1848–9. The event is re-enacted each year. The museum is the richest source of art and artifacts anywhere in the country (see pp34–5).

8 Corvinus University of Budapest

MAP L6 ■ V, Fővám tér 8 ■ 06 482 50 00

A Neo-Renaissance masterpiece, this university was built between 1871 and 1874 to house the city's main customs house. Designed by Miklós Ybl, its Danube façade is set on three levels – a colonnade supporting a balcony, with two rows of arched windows facing the river. The balustrade supports 10 allegorical figures sculpted by August Sommer. The building became the University of Economics in 1951, when it was named after Karl Marx; a statue of Marx still stands in the building. In 2000, it was given its current name.

⑨ Páva Street Synagogue and the Holocaust Memorial Centre

MAP E6 ■ IX, Pava utca 39 ■ 06 455 33 33 ■ Open 10am–6pm Tue–Sun ■ Dis. access ■ Adm ■ www.hdke.hu

Restored and extended between 2002 and 2005 to include the Holocaust Memorial Centre, Páva Street Synagogue was originally built in the 1920s, only to be closed by the then increasingly anti-Semitic Hungarian authorities in 1941. The moving memorial centre includes a number of exhibitions as well as a striking glass Wall of Remembrance on which it is hoped that the name of every Hungarian victim of the Holocaust (there were over 600,000) will be one day be engraved. There are currently around 175,000 names.

The Tree of Life, a Holocaust memorial outside the Great Synagogue

⑩ Great Synagogue

Built in Byzantine style by Viennese architect Ludwig Förster in 1854–9, the largest synagogue in Europe can hold over 3,000 people (see pp36–7). It is home to the Jewish Museum (see p42), which chronicles the long history of the city's Jews. At the rear of the Synagogue is the Raoul Wallenberg Memorial Park, which features the Tree of Life, a Holocaust memorial. Designed by Imre Varga, each leaf of this silver weeping willow tree bears the name of one of the 600,000 Hungarian Jews killed during the Holocaust.

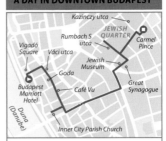

A DAY IN DOWNTOWN BUDAPEST

[Map with labels: Kazinczy utca, JEWISH QUARTER, Rumbach S utca, Carmel Pince, Vigadó Square, Váci utca, Jewish Museum, Goda, Great Synagogue, Budapest Marriott Hotel, Café Vu, Duna (Danube), Inner City Parish Church]

▶ MORNING

A leisurely cup of coffee on the terrace of the Modernist **Budapest Marriott Hotel** (see p116) on Vigadó Square will set the tone for the day. Then walk a short distance east to **Váci utca** (see pp18–19), with its superb retail stores on the northern side, including souvenir stalls, clothes chains and high-end fashion brands. Next, visit Pest's oldest church, the **Inner City Parish Church** (see p89) just off Szabad Sajtó út, before stopping to enjoy a light lunch at **Café Vu** in Mercure Budapest City Center.

AFTERNOON

After lunch, either take the metro from Ferenciek tere up to Astoria or walk ten minutes along the busy Kossuth Lajos utca to the **Great Synagogue** on Dohány utca. You can visit the splendid Byzantine-inspired synagogue and its excellent **Jewish Museum** (see p42) before paying your respects to the Jews killed in the Holocaust at the sobering **Tree of Life** memorial in the **Raoul Wallenberg Memorial Park**, located in the courtyard at the back of the synagogue. Then set about exploring the rest of the fascinating **Jewish Quarter**, which is known for its little gift shops and quaint book stores, as well as the far less ostentatious synagogues on Rumbach S utca and Kazinczy utca. End your day with a delicious glatt-kosher dinner at the **Carmel Pince** restaurant (Kazinczy utca 31).

See map on p88 ←

Cafés and Pubs

① Café Astoria
MAP M4 ▪ V, Kossuth Lajos utca 19–21 ▪ 06 889 60 22 ▪ Open 7am–11pm daily ▪ Dis. access

An elegant café in the Hotel Astoria that manages to turn a cup of coffee into an event.

Opulent interior of Café Astoria

② Gerbeaud Cukrászda
Beautifully decorated cakes complement the interior of the city's most famous café *(see p57)*.

③ Spíler BistroPub
MAP M3 ▪ Király utca 13, Gozsdu udvar ▪ 06 878 13 09

Actually comprises two venues in the Gozsdu Courtyard – Spíler Classic is a gastropub mixing modern design with retro elements of Socialist Hungary, while Spíler Shanghai is more like a secret club in Chinatown.

④ 1000 Tea
MAP L5 ▪ V, Váci utca 65 ▪ 06 337 82 17 ▪ Open noon–9pm Mon–Sat

This café serves a range of teas. With soothing music, it is the perfect place to while away an afternoon.

⑤ Kőleves (Stonesoup)
MAP M3 ▪ VII, Kazinczy utca 37–41 ▪ 06 322 10 11 ▪ Open 11am–midnight

Hearty and healthy fare is served at this reasonably priced restaurant with a citywide reputation. Wash it all down with one of their house wines.

⑥ Blue Lagoon Tiki Bar
MAP M5 ▪ V, Szerb utca 17 ▪ 0670 594 33 55 ▪ Open 4pm–midnight daily (to 1am Fri)

Possibly Budapest's cheapest cocktail bar. The Hawaiian kitsch-fest decor is unashamedly over-the-top, but the locals and visitors who pack the place out wouldn't have it any other way.

⑦ Szimpla Kert
In a refurbished apartment block, Szimpla Kert is the biggest ruined-garden bar in the seventh district. It's also one of the most popular pubs in town, with frequent concerts *(see p56)*.

⑧ Centrál Kávéház
MAP L4 ▪ V, Károlyi Mihály utca 9 ▪ 06 266 21 10 ▪ Dis. access

On the site of an 1880s coffee shop, Centrál Kávéház is a local favourite.

⑨ Paris, Texas
MAP D5 ▪ IX, Ráday utca 22 ▪ 06 218 05 70 ▪ Open noon–3am

A late-night hotspot of the city's trendy set, who like to stop for a nightcap on their way home. The Texan link is reinforced by the large range of malt whiskies on offer.

⑩ Doblo
Fine wines from all over the world can be sampled at this elegant little bar. The emphasis is naturally on local wines, but you can select from an extensive international list. The knowledgeable staff are happy to make suggestions *(see p56)*.

Customers enjoy fine wines at Doblo

Restaurants

1 Apostolok
MAP L4 ▪ V, Kígyó utca 4–6
▪ 06 269 95 66 ▪ FFF

This restaurant in the heart of the
city opened as a pub in 1902. It offers
excellent food showcasing traditional
Hungarian flavours.

2 Kádár Étkezde
MAP D4 ▪ VII, Klauzál tér 9
▪ 06 321 36 22 ▪ Open 11:30am–
3:30pm Tue–Sat ▪ No credit cards ▪ F

This non-kosher Hungarian Jewish
eatery in the seventh district is an
authentic neighbourhood treasure.

3 Costes
White-gloved waiters glide
from table to table at this chic,
Michelin-starred restaurant that's
at the forefront of Budapest's
contemporary fine-dining scene. It's
not for the budget-conscious, though
the lunch menu is cheaper *(see p54)*.

4 Baraka
Contemporary in both design
and cuisine Baraka offers several
well-priced tasting menus (up to
seven courses), which allows you to
fully experience the flavours coming
out of the kitchen. The accompanying
wine list is outstanding *(see p54)*.

5 Comme Chez Soi
Fine Italian cuisine makes up
the menu at this charming little
place. All food is prepared in an open
kitchen behind the bar, so diners can
see their meals taking shape. It's not
cheap, and you will need to reserve
a table a day or two in advance,
but its worth both the cost and the
wait. A really fantastic culinary
experience *(see p54)*.

6 Cyrano
MAP K4 ▪ V, Kristóf tér 7–8
▪ 06 226 47 47 ▪ Open 8am–midnight
daily ▪ Dis. access ▪ FFF

Said to serve the best goulash soup in
town, luxurious Cyrano is renowned
for its consistently high standards.

7 Kárpátia Étterem és Söröző
MAP L4 ▪ V, Ferenciek tere 7–8 ▪ 06 317
35 96 ▪ Open 11am–11pm daily ▪ Dis.
access ▪ FFF

Classic dishes in historic surroundings
at one of the city's top restaurants.

Galleried interior at Borbíróság

8 Borbíróság
MAP M6 ▪ IX, Csarnoktér 5
▪ 06 219 09 02 ▪ Open noon–
11:30pm Mon–Sat ▪ FF

The "law courts of wine" venue has a
legal theme and a vast array of mainly
Hungarian wines on offer.

9 Múzeum Kávéház és Étterem
MAP M4 ▪ VIII, Múzeum körút 12
▪ 06 338 42 21 ▪ Open 6pm–
midnight Mon–Sat ▪ Dis. access ▪ FFF

This 1855 former coffee house is next
to the National Museum and serves
delicious Hungarian specialities.

10 Babel
MAP L4 ▪ V, Piarista köz 2
▪ 0670 600 08 00 ▪ Open 6pm–
midnight Tue–Sat ▪ Dis. access ▪ FFF

At the foot of the Elizabeth Bridge,
this bistro/delicatessen offers fresh
ingredients and attentive service.

See map on p88

TOP 10 Around Városliget

Home to some of the finest buildings and widest boulevards in the city, the area around Városliget (City Park) is where the citizens of Budapest have long come to play. Everything is built on a gloriously grand scale, from the cafés and bistros of Liszt Ferenc tér to the mansions of Andrássy út and Városligeti fasor, and even the City Park itself – fronted by the magnificent Millennium Monument. Városliget was chosen as the centre of the city's 1896 Millennium Celebrations (see p96), and among the many splendid buildings constructed especially for the event were the Museum of Fine Arts and Vajdahunyad Castle.

Detail of the Millennium Monument

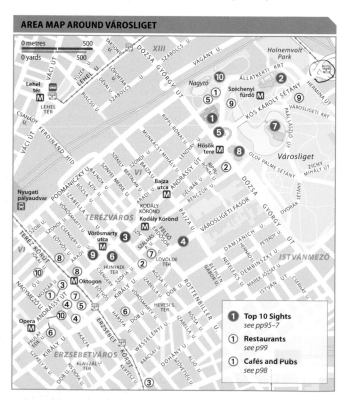

AREA MAP AROUND VÁROSLIGET

1 Top 10 Sights
see pp95–7

1 Restaurants
see p99

1 Cafés and Pubs
see p98

1 Museum of Fine Arts
MAP E2 ■ XIV, Hősök tere, Dózsa György út 41 ■ 06 469 71 00 ■ Closed for renovation until 2018 ■ Dis. access ■ www.szepmuveszeti.hu

Hungary's largest collection of international art is housed in a 1906 building designed by Fülöp Herzog and Albert Schikendanz. It has works by Raphael, Goya and Velázquez, and the largest collection of El Grecos outside Spain. It shares its collection with the National Gallery (see pp26–7).

Outdoor pools, Széchenyi Baths

2 Széchenyi Baths
MAP F2 ■ XIV, Állatkerti út 11 ■ 06 363 32 10 ■ Open May–Sep: 6am–10pm daily (steam and thermal baths close at 7pm) ■ Adm ■ www.budapestspas.hu

Opened in 1913, Széchenyi is a vast complex of indoor and outpoor pools, which include Hungary's deepest and hottest thermal baths. Immensely popular all year round, this is where people come to find the classic Hungarian bathing experience.

3 Andrássy Street
MAP L2, M2

A long, wide boulevard from Városliget to the city centre, Andrássy út is Budapest's most exclusive address. It is lined with restaurants, theatres and shops, as well as the State Opera (see pp32–3). At No. 22 is the Drechsler Palace, built by the Hungarian Railways as rental apartments for its pension fund in 1883, before being used later as the Hungarian Ballet Academy. The building is currently empty, but there are plans to turn it into a luxury hotel. The House of Terror Museum (see p97) is further down the street, at No. 60. Under Andrássy út runs the Metro 1, Hungary's oldest and the world's second-oldest underground railway. It was declared a UNESCO World Heritage Site in 2002.

4 Városligeti Avenue
MAP E3

This serene tree-lined avenue is the gentle counterpart to the more commercial Andrássy út. Numerous embassies line the avenue, and there are two significant churches in the street: a Calvinist one at the southern end and a Lutheran one towards Városliget.

5 Heroes' Square
MAP E2 ■ Hősök tere

Heroes' Square was laid out during the 1890s and was the focal point of Hungary's Millennium Celebrations in 1896 (held to mark 1,000 years since the Magyar conquest of the Carpathian Basin). At its heart is the 36-m (110-ft) Millennium Monument, flanked by two colonnades. The riders on horseback at the foot of the monument represent the seven chieftains of the seven Magyar tribes that settled in Hungary.

Millennium Monument

Pianos in the Franz Liszt Museum

6 Franz Liszt Museum

MAP D3 ■ VI, Vörösmarty utca 35 ■ 06 322 98 04 ■ Open 10am–6pm Mon–Fri, 9am–5pm Sat ■ Adm ■ www.lisztmuseum.hu

More famously known to the world by his Germanic name of Franz, Ferenc Liszt was Hungary's greatest composer. He lived here from 1881 until his death in 1886. The house became a museum in 1986 and the furniture, pianos and manuscripts give an insight into the life and work of this extraordinary man.

7 Vajdahunyad Castle

MAP F2 ■ Museum of Agriculture: 06 363 11 17; open Apr–Oct: 10am–5pm daily; Nov–Mar: 10am–4pm Tue–Fri, 10am–5pm Sat & Sun; adm

In the middle of Városliget is the incredible Vajdahunyad Castle, a mixture of Renaissance, Gothic, Baroque and Romanesque styles, designed by Ignác Alpár for the Millennium Celebrations. Alpár's idea was to illustrate

> **THE MILLENNIUM EXHIBITION**
>
> Much of Városliget, including the monument that marks its entrance, was built for the 1896 Millennium Exhibition, which celebrated 1,000 years since Árpád inhabited the area near Budapest. Besides the monuments around Városliget, the exhibition saw the opening of the millennium metro line – Continental Europe's first – the installation of the city's first gas lights, and the construction of an enormous number of Secessionist buildings.

the entire evolution of Hungarian architecture in a single construction. To achieve this, each section reflects an important edifice and, all in all, the castle represents more than 20 famous Hungarian buildings. The Museum of Agriculture in the Baroque section is the only part of the castle that is open to the public.

8 Műcsarnok (Kunsthalle)

MAP E2 ■ XIV, Hősök tere ■ 06 460 70 00 ■ Open 10am–6pm Tue–Sun, noon–8pm Thu ■ Dis. access ■ Adm ■ www.mucsarnok.hu

Facing the Museum of Fine Arts, the Műcsarnok (literally "art hall") was completed in 1895. The imposing building, dominated by its portico with six supporting columns, was designed by Fülöp Herzog and Albert Schikendanz. Today, it hosts temporary exhibitions and concerts.

Vajdahunyad Castle

9 House of Terror Museum

MAP D3 ■ VI, Andrássy út 60 ■ 06 374 26 00 ■ Open 10am–6pm Tue–Sun ■ Adm ■ www.terrorhaza.hu

This building was the headquarters of the fascist Arrow Cross before and during World War II, and the secret police afterwards. Exhibits include a T54 tank used in the repression of the 1956 revolution. In the basement, used as a prison during both regimes, one cell has been recreated to look just as it did in the 1940s.

House of Terror Museum

10 Budapest Zoo

MAP E2 ■ XIV, Városliget, Állatkerti körút 6–12 ■ 06 273 49 00 ■ Open May–Aug: 9am–5pm Mon–Thu, 9am–6pm Fri–Sun; Apr & Sep: 9am–4:30pm Mon–Thu, 9am–5pm Fri–Sun; Mar & Oct: 9am–5pm Mon–Thu, 9am–4:30pm Fri–Sun ■ Dis. access ■ Adm ■ www.zoobudapest.com

Established in 1866, the city's zoo is considered one of the best in Central Europe, and is known for its large primate house. The animal enclosures mostly mimic their natural habitat. There is a children's zoo where tamer animals can be petted, and various shows are held twice a day. Most of the zoo's animal houses are listed buildings, built in late Secessionist style between 1909 and 1911.

A DAY IN VÁROSLIGET

MORNING

Városliget is a great place for a family outing. Start off early with a dip in Budapest's most popular thermal baths, **Széchenyi** *(see p95)*, situated right in the middle of Városliget with its own metro station on the Lilliputian Millennium line. Refreshed, you can then take the kids next door to the **Budapest Zoo**, to admire both animals and buildings. You can get information about the programmes for the day at the entrance. After the trip to the zoo, take a walk around the park's lake at Kós Károly sétány. For hot Hungarian dishes, sausages and fresh beer, visit **Városligeti Sörsátor** *(see p98)*, located amidst the trees in the City Park.

AFTERNOON

Start the afternoon off at the **Museum of Fine Arts** *(see p95)* at the edge of the park in **Heroes' Square**. Although you could spend all afternoon here, try to restrict yourself to an hour and a half, but don't miss the Raphael *Madonna* or the fabulous collection of El Grecos. Then give the kids a treat by taking them to see the model buildings and railways at **Miniversum** *(see p52)* before heading back to the park to admire the architecture of **Vajdahunyad Castle**, ideally from a rowing boat on the park's central lake. If you are visiting in winter, you can go ice-skating on the lake *(see p53)*. Finally, end the day with a superb family dinner at **Robinson** *(see p99)*, one of Budapest's most famous restaurants.

See map on p94

Cafés and Pubs

Elegant Art Deco-style interior at the New York Café és Étterem

1 Caledonia
MAP M1 ▪ VI, Mozsár utca 9
▪ 06 311 76 11 ▪ Open 11am–midnight
Mon–Thu, 11am–1am Fri & Sat

This friendly Scottish pub serves some very hearty meals. With a number of big screens, it's a great place to catch an important sporting event.

2 Mirage Café & Bar
MAP E2 ▪ VI, Dózsa György út 88 ▪ 06 462 70 70 ▪ Open 10am–10pm daily

The location opposite Heroes' Square pulls in the crowds, but the food and prices are good for a tourist hotspot.

3 New York Café és Étterem
Sip your hot chocolate or martini under the cherub-adorned ceiling at this Budapest institution *(see p59)*.

4 Menza
MAP M2 ▪ VI, Liszt Ferenc tér 2 ▪ 06 413 14 82 ▪ Open 10am–midnight daily

Restaurant and coffee house with a retro design and a modern take on Magyar canteen favourites.

5 Café Vian
Coffee, cocktails, pasta and salads make Vian a one-stop shop. Enjoy the view out on the terrace and watch the world go by at this ever-busy café *(see p57)*.

6 Sugar Shop
MAP M2 ▪ Paulay Ede utca 48
▪ 06 321 66 72 ▪ Open 10am–10pm daily

Give in to the irresistible, colourful sweets at this confectionery and candy shop. *Tejberizs* (milk rice pudding) is a local favourite.

7 Ferdinand Monarchy Czech Beerhouse
MAP D2 ▪ Szív út 30 ▪ 06 312 20 77
▪ Open noon–11pm daily

Reminiscent of Prague, serving speciality beers from the Czech Republic.

8 Hello Baby
MAP D3 ▪ VI, Andrássy út 52 ▪ 06 776 07 67 ▪ Open 10pm–5am Fri & Sat

This club attracts a slightly older, less touristy crowd than other places in the area. With two separate dance floors, there's a choice of music.

9 Városligeti Sörsátor
MAP F2 ▪ XIV, Kós Károly sétány
▪ 0670 599 36 25 ▪ Open 11am–10pm daily

Hungarian beer house where drinking is taken very seriously. Wine served directly from barrels is also available.

10 Két Szerecsen
MAP D3 ▪ Nagymező utca 14
▪ 06 343 19 84 ▪ Open daily

This bistro has excellent food, coffee and an extensive wine menu.

Restaurants

1 Gundel
MAP E2 ▪ Gundel Károly út 4
▪ 06 889 81 11 ▪ Open noon–midnight
▪ Dis. access ▪ www.gundel.hu ▪ FFF
Probably Hungary's most famous
restaurant and one of the priciest.
Traditional yet creative food.

2 Haxen Király
MAP D3 ▪ VI, Király utca 100
▪ 06 351 67 93 ▪ Open noon–
midnight daily ▪ FFF
This Teutonic eatery is known for its
wurst with sauerkraut. Lederhosen-
attired men play the accordion.

3 The Big Fish
MAP D3 ▪ VI, Andrássy út 44
▪ 06 269 06 93 ▪ Open noon–10pm
daily ▪ FFF
Pick what you like from the extensive
fresh seafood counter and have it
cooked just as you wish.

The Big Fish seafood counter

4 Seasons Bistro
MAP M2 ▪ VI, Liszt Ferenc
tér 7 ▪ 06 709 24 68 ▪ Open 11am–
midnight daily ▪ FF
This restaurant is known for steaks,
prepared using special equipment.
Wide selection of wines and beers.

5 Bagolyvár
MAP E2 ▪ XIV, Gundel Károly
út 2 ▪ 06 468 31 10 ▪ Open noon–
11pm daily ▪ FF
A family-friendly restaurant serving
traditional Hungarian food is set in
an atmospheric dark-beamed villa.

6 Maharaja
MAP D3 ▪ VII, Csengery utca 24
▪ 06 351 12 89 ▪ Open noon–11pm
daily ▪ Dis. access ▪ FF
Family-run Maharaja presents
authentic curries that are subtly
spiced and delicious.

7 Trattoria Gusto
MAP M2 ▪ VI, Liszt Ferenc
tér 11 ▪ 06 321 84 25 ▪ Open noon–
midnight daily ▪ FF
Clay-oven pizzas and other Italian
favourites are dished up in a pretty
high-ceilinged dining room.

8 Arriba Taqueria
MAP D3 ▪ VI, Teréz körút 25
▪ 06 374 00 57 ▪ Open 11am–10pm
daily (to 11pm Fri, Sat) ▪ F
Although essentially just fast food,
served at the counter, this is the best
Tex-Mex eatery in Budapest.

9 Robinson
MAP E2 ▪ XIV, Városligeti-tó
(City Park Lake) ▪ 06 422 02 22
▪ Open daily ▪ Dis. access ▪ FF
Located on a tiny island, this place
serves seafood in an informal setting.

**10 Parázs Presszo Thai
Restaurant**
MAP D3 ▪ Jókai utca 8 ▪ 06 950 37 70
▪ Open noon–midnight daily ▪ FF
A small restaurant perfect for lovers
of authentic spicy Thai food.

See map on p94

TOP10 Greater Budapest

While the city centre has enough to keep most visitors happy for weeks, Budapest's suburbs have now spread out almost endlessly into the surrounding Pannonian plains and incorporate some extraordinary sights. These include the former Roman city of Aquincum, today bordered by a train line and a highway, as well as the former Roman garrison at Óbuda to the southwest. The Buda Hills, once some distance from the city, now have villas and apartment blocks in their foothills, while the remarkable limestone caves at Pálvölgy and Szemlő-hegy are almost lost in the city's urban sprawl.

Worker's Movement Memorial, Memento Park

AREA MAP OF GREATER BUDAPEST

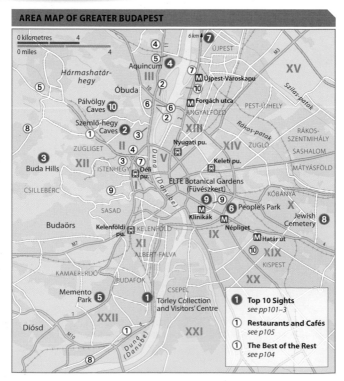

① **Top 10 Sights**
see pp101–3

① **Restaurants and Cafés**
see p105

① **The Best of the Rest**
see p104

1 Törley Collection and Visitors' Centre

MAP P3 ■ XXII, Anna utca 5–7

Widely recognized as the father of the Hungarian wine industry, József Törley studied the art of wine-making in Reims, the Champagne capital of France. He returned to Hungary in the 1880s, and set about producing superb sparkling wine in Budafok, a Budapest suburb. The Törley Collection displays the long and tumultuous history of Törley sparkling wines. With clear Ottoman influences, the architecture is also a major highlight of the centre.

Törley Collection exhibition

2 Szemlő-hegy Caves

MAP N1 ■ II, Pusztaszeri út 35 ■ 06 325 60 01 ■ Open 10am–4pm Wed–Mon ■ Adm

Known to many as the city of thermal waters, Budapest is also known for its caves. North of the city centre are the Pilis Hills, home to several fabulous cave systems. The Szemlő-hegy Caves are the closest to the city, on bus route No. 11 from Batthyány tér to Pusztaszeri út (it's about a mile walk from there). The caves feature splendid formations known as cave pearls that resemble bunches of grapes growing out of the rock. These are produced by the action of hot springs penetrating limestone. The air here is said to be therapeutic for bronchial infections.

3 Buda Hills

MAP N1

The forested Buda Hills to the west of the city make an ideal getaway (see p103). The best way to reach them is to take the Cogwheel Railway (see p52), which begins at Városmajor. At the top, a short walk leads to the huge TV tower. The Children's Railway (see p52) begins at the base of the tower and meanders through the Buda Hills to its terminus at Hűvös Valley. En route is the Elizabeth Lookout Tower (Erzsébet-kilátó), which has a chairlift that takes you back to Buda. It was constructed by Frigyes Schulek in 1910, but the purpose for which it was built remains a mystery.

4 Aquincum

MAP P1 ■ III, Szentendrei út 139 ■ 06 250 16 50, 06 454 04 38 ■ Open: Apr–Oct: 10am–6pm Tue–Sun; May–Sep: 10am–6pm Tue–Sun (ruins from 9am); Nov–Mar: 10am–4pm Tue–Sun (ruins only in good weather) ■ Dis. access ■ Adm

The capital of the Roman province of Pannonia, Aquincum was for centuries the largest city in Central Europe. Excavated in the 19th century, it is one of the city's most popular sights. The outlines of streets and buildings are clearly visible. The museum, inside a Neo-Classical Lapidarium, houses Roman artifacts found at the site and models showing what the town once looked like.

Ruins of ancient Aquincum

Sculpture in Memento Park

5 Memento Park
MAP N3 ▪ XXII, Balatoni út
▪ 06 424 75 00 ▪ Open 10am–sunset
daily ▪ Adm ▪ www.mementopark.hu

The grounds of Memento Park bring together over 40 examples of the Communist-era statues and placques (some astonishingly huge) that once stood in public spaces all over Budapest. Marx, Engels and Lenin are all present, as is the Stalin pedestal, complete with a full-scale replica of his boots: these were all that remained when Stalin's statue was toppled and destroyed during the 1956 revolution. There's also a Trabant – known as "the people's car" – on show, while multimedia displays in a barracks-style building reveal some of the cunning methods the AVH, the Hungarian secret police, used to spy on their own people. There are buses to the park from Déak tér at 11am each day.

6 People's Park
MAP P2 ▪ VIII, Népliget

The city's largest park, Népliget was laid out in the 1860s and covers an area of 112 ha (277 acres). It has large tracts of grass and trees, as well as flower beds and playgrounds. It is also home to Budapest's Planetarium (see p53). Népliget was also the site of the city's first motor racing track, and even hosted a Grand Prix in 1936, when Tazio Nuvolari won in his Alfa Romeo. The track fell into disuse after 1972 and, when Hungary decided to host Formula One in the 1980s, a new track, Hungaroring, was built outside town.

7 Aquaworld
MAP D3 ▪ IV, Ives út 16
▪ 06 231 37 60 ▪ Open 6am–10pm
daily ▪ Dis. access ▪ Adm ▪ www.
aquaworldresort.hu

An enormous waterpark with pools, wave machines, slides, artificial beaches, saunas and playgrounds, Aquaworld is a great family day out. Some slides are four or five storeys high and almost 1 km (half a mile) in length. Much of the park is under cover, but some of the attractions are outdoors, and some of the slides have minimum height restrictions.

8 Jewish Cemetery
MAP Q2 ▪ XVII, Kozma utca
▪ Open 8am–3pm Sun–Fri (summer: to 4pm)

Opened in 1893 and full of wonderfully elaborate tombs, this cemetery is a stark reminder of the wealth and influence wielded by Budapest's Jews before World War II. Some of the tombs were designed by leading architects, including Ödön Lechner and Gyula Fodor.

THE MARVELLOUS MAGYARS

It may seem far-fetched, but Hungary once had the most gifted football team in the world. The legendary Ferenc Puskás led Real Madrid to three of their five European Cup triumphs after defecting to Spain. In November 1953, Hungary achieved a legendary 6–3 win over England at Wembley Stadium (below). The English press dubbed them the "Marvellous Magyars" and Puskás the "Galloping Major" as he was once a major in the Hungarian army.

⑨ ELTE Botanical Garden (Füvészkert)

MAP F6 ■ VIII, Illés utca 25
■ Open Nov–Mar: 9am–4pm daily;
Apr–Oct: 10am–5pm daily ■ Adm

Spread over 3 ha (8 acres) in eastern Budapest, the ELTE Botanical Garden offers splendid relief from the bustle of the city centre. The gardens are part of ELTE University, though they were first laid out by the Festetics family, who lived in the Neo-Classical villa that is now the administration centre. They are renowned for their palm trees.

Visitors admire the Pálvölgy Caves

⑩ Pálvölgy Caves

MAP N1 ■ II, Szépvölgyi út 162
■ 06 325 95 05 ■ Open 10am–4pm
Tue–Sun ■ Adm ■ no children under 5

A hut at the foot of a steep cliff marks the entrance to the Pálvölgy Caves. As well as the cave pearl formations that are also found in Szemlő-hegy, Pálvölgy is known for its formations that are said to resemble animals. Though many of the caves are accessible, and can be visited via stairs and galleries, several of the more spectacular formations can only be seen by joining a guided tour. Wear warm clothes as the temperatures inside the caves can be chilly.

A DAY IN THE BUDA HILLS

▶ MORNING

Start the day by taking bus No. 291 from Nyugati Pu to its terminus at the foot of the Libegő (chairlift), which gently takes you up to the summit of **János Hill**. From here, it is a short walk to the **Children's Railway** *(see p52)*, a splendid relic of Hungary's Communist past. As the train meanders through the hills, you can stop off and climb to the top of the extraordinary **Elizabeth Lookout Tower** *(see p101)* for sensational views of the city below. Then take the steam train, which leaves on the hour throughout summer. Get off at **Szépjuhászné Station** and try the station's super outdoor café for lunch.

AFTERNOON

Set off on a well-marked path to the **Budakeszi Wildlife Park** (0623 45 17 83; www.vadaspark-budakeszi.hu). Occupying an area of 327 ha (808 acres), it has a wide variety of animals to see, from wild boars – which also roam freely in the surrounding countryside – to packs of wolves. There is also a separate reserve for plantlife. Take the park's walking safari tour to visit its best sections and enjoy climbing in the adventure park. The park's own restaurant is a great place for dinner, serving generous amounts of traditional local food and Hungarian wine, and there is lively folk music and dancing every evening after 6pm. As the Children's Railway will almost certainly be closed by the time you finish eating, you can take bus No. 22 to Széll Kálmán tér. From there, you can get the metro back to the centre of the city.

See map on p100 ←

The Best of the Rest

① Tropicarium-Oceanarium

MAP N3 ▪ XXII, Nagytétényí út 37–45 ▪ 06 424 30 53 ▪ Open 10am–8pm daily ▪ Adm ▪ www.tropicarium.hu

You can stare into the eyes of a shark or touch a snake at this aquarium and indoor tropical rainforest.

Displays at the Kassák Museum

② Kassák Museum

MAP P1 ▪ III, Fő tér 1 ▪ 06 368 70 21 ▪ Open 10am–5pm Wed–Sun ▪ Adm

Housed in Zichy Palace, this museum showcases the works of avant-garde artist Lajos Kassák.

③ Óbuda Amphitheatre

MAP N1 ▪ III, Bécsi út

Dating from around AD 140–150, the military amphitheatre is the larger of Budapest's two Roman amphitheatres, and still has two arched entrances as well as tunnels from where wild animals entered.

④ Aquincum Amphitheatre

MAP P1 ▪ III, Szentendrei út

Once packed with 10,000 spectators, Aquincum's civil amphitheatre lies sandwiched between the HÉV railway and a main road. It was built around AD 250–300 (see p101).

⑤ Aqueduct

MAP P1 ▪ III, Szentendrei út

A restored section of the 2nd-century aqueduct that carried water from Óbuda to Aquincum lies to the east of Szentendrei út. Traffic runs along either side, so take care.

⑥ Hungarian Museum of Trade and Tourism

MAP P1 ▪ III, Korona tér 1 ▪ 06 375 62 49 ▪ Open 10am–6pm Tue–Sat ▪ Adm

Explore the history of Hungarian catering and home cuisine, and learn to cook some traditional dishes.

⑦ Hospital in the Rock Nuclear Bunker Museum

MAP N2 ▪ I, Lovas út 4/c ▪ 0670 701 01 01 ▪ Open 10am–8pm daily ▪ Adm

Wax figures bring to life the eerie history of the system of caverns under Buda Castle, an emergency hospital and shelter from World War II that became a nuclear bunker by 1962.

⑧ Nagytétény Palace

MAP N3 ▪ XXII, Kastélypark utca 9–11 ▪ 06 207 00 55 ▪ Opening times vary ▪ Adm

A design museum featuring classic furniture, housed in one of Hungary's best Baroque palaces.

⑨ Ludovika Academy

MAP P2 ▪ X, Ludovika tér 2–6 ▪ 06 210 10 85 ▪ Open 10am–5pm Wed–Sun ▪ Dis. access ▪ Adm ▪ www.nhmus.hu

Part of this former military school is home to the Natural History Museum.

⑩ Wekerle Estate

MAP P2 ▪ XIX, Kós Károly tér

Central Europe's first Garden City was inspired by Transylvania's Saxon villages. Homes here are sought after.

Home on the Wekerle Estate

Restaurants and Cafés

PRICE CATEGORIES

For a three-course meal for one, with half
a bottle of wine (or equivalent meal),
taxes and extra charges.

F under Ft5,000   **FF** Ft5,000–10,000
FFF over Ft10,000

1 Remiz
MAP N1 ■ II, Budakeszi út 5
■ 06 275 13 96 ■ Open noon–11pm
daily ■ FFF

Good Hungarian food and wine, plus
Budapest's best rack of ribs. There's
also a lovely garden, perfect for
dining alfresco in nice weather.

2 Kéhli
MAP P1 ■ III, Mókus utca 22
■ 06 250 42 41 ■ Open daily ■ Dis.
access ■ FF

Founded in 1899, Kéhli serves good
old-fashioned Hungarian food, with a
live folk band that plays most nights.

3 Fióka
MAP N2 ■ XII, Városmajor utca
75 ■ 06 426 55 55 ■ Open 11am–
midnight daily ■ FF

This former post office is now a
charming gastropub serving lots
of game and very good local wines.

4 Kispéntek
MAP A3 ■ II, Retek utca 12
■ 0630 384 22 40 ■ Open 11:30am–
10pm Mon–Sat ■ FF

The menu covers everything from
Chinese noodles to American salads,
and manages to get it all just right.

5 Náncsi Néni
MAP N1 ■ II, Ördögárok út 80
■ 06 397 27 42 ■ Open daily ■ Dis.
access ■ F

Fantastic regional dishes that only
use farm-fresh ingredients.

6 Zöld Kapu Vendéglő
MAP P1 ■ III, Szőlő utca 42
■ Open 10am–10pm daily ■ FF

A traditional Hungarian restaurant
with a charming garden, serving

huge portions of hearty food in the
middle of Óbuda.

7 Központ Bisztró
MAP P1 ■ IV, Szent István tér 1
■ 0620 374 97 85 ■ Open 8am–10pm
Mon–Sat, 10am–10pm Sun ■ F

Popular with the locals for their
burgers and international cuisine.
Near Újpest-Központ metro station.

Interior of Budai Gesztenyés

8 Budai Gesztenyés
MAP N2 ■ Budakeszi, Szana-
tórium utca 2 ■ 0623 45 05 34
■ Open 11am–11pm daily ■ FF

Modern European food with a
Hungarian twist. There are just a
few options for each course. Given
the high quality, prices are a steal.

9 Jardinette
MAP N2 ■ XII, Németvölgyi út
136 ■ 06 248 16 52 ■ Open Tue–Sun
■ Dis. access ■ FF

Exquisite French food served in a
lovely garden. The wine list is superb.

10 Eat & Meet
MAP P1 ■ XIII, Danubius utca
14 ■ 06 517 51 80 ■ Open 6:30–11pm
Sat, Sun ■ FF

A local family serves dinner in an
apartment overlooking the Danube.
The food is authentically Hungarian
and the family dines with you.

See map on p100

Streetsmart

Picturesque buildings in the
Castle Hill district of Buda

Getting To and Around Budapest

Arriving by Air

Hungary has not had a national airline for some time, but over 40 international airlines now fly to Budapest's only airport, **Liszt Ferenc International**. Flights from London take around 2 hours, while those from New York take about 9 hours.

The airport's terminals offer a wide range of retail outlets, dining options and many other services. There are currency exchange bureaux and car rental companies including **Avis**, **Europcar**, **Hertz** and **Sixt**.

Liszt Ferenc airport lies about 16 km (10 miles) southwest of the main city centre.

For around Ft3,900 the Airport Shuttle Minibus (**miniBUD**) will take you to the city centre, although you may have to wait for other passengers to assemble.

Airport taxis will drive you anywhere in the city for a flat fee of around Ft6,500, which you will need to pay in advance. There is also a public bus, identified by its 200E Reptér Busz sign, which runs to Kőbánya-Kispest metro station, from where the M3 metro line runs into the city centre.

Arriving by Train

Budapest has rail connections to more than 25 other capital cities, and it has a busy and efficient internal network. There are three stations – one

in Buda and two in Pest – and each has links to the metro system.

Keleti is Hungary's biggest railway station, serving the eastern region of Hungary as well as most international destinations. The station is about 3 km (2 miles) east of the city centre, on metro lines M2 and M4.

The station closest to the city centre is Nyugati, but it only provides train services to the Hungarian countryside. Metro line M3 stops here. Kelenföld, on metro line M4, serves Lake Balaton and western Hungary.

Arriving by Road

All international coaches arrive at Népliget Bus Station in southern Pest, which is close to Népliget metro station on line M3. Budapest is 250 km (155 miles) from Vienna, and the M1 motorway brings you within the city limits in just 3 hours. Since Hungary joined the Schengen group of nations it has become easier to drive here, as there are now only cursory passport checks – if any at all – at the borders with Austria, Slovenia and Slovakia, and quick, routine checks at Romania and Croatia. However, expect long delays at the border with Serbia and the Ukraine.

Arriving by Boat

Arriving in Budapest by boat is perhaps the most stylish way to make your

entrance into the city. During the summer, there are hydrofoil services to and from Vienna and Bratislava, which arrive at Vigadó tér (see p48). The journey time from Vienna is just under 3 hours.

Getting Around by Metro

Budapest has mainland Europe's oldest metro system. The M1 line, with its tiny stations and three-carriage trains, opened in 1896 and is a tourist attraction in itself. There are four metro lines in all, which serve most of Pest, though little of Buda. Lines M2 and M4 run from east to west, while the M3 line runs from north to south and serves Kőbánya-Kispest for the airport. Trains on all lines run from 4:30am to 11:10pm.

In addition to the metro, Budapest boasts five HÉV suburban lines. These are good for visiting sights outside of town, including Szentendre, Aquincum, Gödöllő, Hungaroring and Ráckeve.

Getting Around by Bus

Buses are plentiful in Budapest and are a very good option in the city centre, running all day and night. Most major roads benefit from three or four bus routes. Destination and route information is clearly displayed at all stops.

Getting Around by Tram

Budapest has an extensive tram network with over 30 lines, a number of which cross the river and link both parts of the city. Note, however, that many trams and some buses are not accessible to people in wheelchairs.

Public Transport Tickets

Single tickets cost Ft350 and are valid on all metro lines, buses and trams, and the HÉV within Budapest's city limits. They can be bought at the airport, train stations and metro stations, as well as at kiosks close to major bus stops, or from ticket-vending machines found at most main transport stops. Single tickets can also be bought direct from bus drivers, for Ft450. Tickets need to be franked at the entrance to the metro, or on board buses and trams. If you transfer from one metro line to another, or change buses or trams, you will need to validate a new ticket. You can buy a book of 10 tickets for Ft3,000, but the best value option for visitors is the 24-hour Travelcard, which costs Ft1,650. You can also buy a Budapest Card, valid for 48 hours or 72 hours, which offers free transport and free or reduced priced entry at a number of the city's attractions.

Getting Around on Foot

Perhaps the best way of getting around Budapest is on foot. Many central areas are pedestrianized – this includes Váci utca and the Castle District. The Danube Embankment is also a great place for a leisurely stroll, and rewards walkers with stunning views.

Getting Around by Taxi

There are several taxi companies operating in Budapest; however, all licensed taxis are yellow and are obliged to use the same pricing, calculated mainly on the distance. Although you can hail taxis or take one at a taxi station, it is recommended to call one by phone or by using a smartphone app.

Getting Around by Car

This is the least convenient method of getting around Budapest. There are very few places to park (almost none at all in the city centre), the traffic is terrible, and the maze of one-way systems can make the city a forbidding place for the uninitiated driver. The speed limit in built-up areas is 50 km/h (30 mph), and it is illegal to drive after consuming any alcohol. Penalties for offenders are high.

Getting Around by Boat

A number of river boat companies run services along the Danube during the summer. Most of them call in at all of the city's jetties on both sides of the river, as well as at Margaret Island, with Vigadó tér acting as the main terminus.

DIRECTORY

AIRPORT

Liszt Ferenc International Airport
℡ 06 296 96 96; 06 296 70 00
ⓦ bud.hu

miniBUD
℡ 06 550 00 00
ⓦ minibud.hu

TRAIN INFORMATION

MÁV (Hungarian Railways)
℡ 06 444 44 99 (24 hrs)
ⓦ mav-start.hu

COACH INFORMATION

Coach Bookings
℡ 06 382 08 88; 06 219 80 86
ⓦ volanbusz.hu

PUBLIC TRANSPORT INFORMATION
ⓦ bkk.hu/en

CAR RENTALS

Avis
℡ 06 318 42 40
ⓦ avis.com

Europcar
℡ 06 204 29 94
ⓦ europcar.com

Hertz
℡ 06 296 09 99
ⓦ hertz.hu

Sixt
℡ 06 451 42 27
ⓦ sixt.com

BOAT SERVICES

Mahart Passnave
℡ 06 484 40 00
ⓦ mahartpassnave.hu

TAXI COMPANIES

Budapest Taxi
℡ 06 777 77 77

Citytaxi
℡ 06 211 11 11

Green Taxi
℡ 06 400 00 00

RIVER BOAT TOURS

Legenda River Cruises
℡ 06 317 22 03
ⓦ legenda.hu

RiverRide
℡ 06 332 25 55
ⓦ riverride.com

Practical Information

Passports and Visas

Citizens of all the other European Union (EU) and European Economic Area (EEA) countries may enter Hungary without a visa and stay for as long as they please, although they are legally obliged to register as residents with the local authorities after staying 90 days. US, Canadian, Australian and New Zealand citizens, and citizens of Schengen member states, may also enter without a visa and stay for 90 days. Citizens of all other countries should check entry requirements with a Hungarian consulate before travelling: visas cannot be issued at Budapest airport (or indeed any border point), and travellers without the correct paperwork will be turned away.

Customs Regulations

If arriving from outside the EU, besides personal belongings you can bring the following items into the country – 40 cigarettes, four litres of wine, one litre of spirits and €300 worth of gifts. There are no limits on the import of goods from EU countries.

Travel Safety Advice

Visitors can get up-to-date safety information from the **Foreign and Commonwealth Office (FCO)** in the UK, the **State Department** in the US and the **Department of Foreign Affairs and Trade** in Australia.

Travel Insurance

All travellers are advised to buy insurance against accidents, illness, theft or loss and travel delays or cancellations. Hungary has a reciprocal health agreement with other EU countries, and EU citizens receive emergency treatment under the public healthcare system if they have with them a valid European Health Insurance Card (EHIC). Prescriptions must be paid for upfront. Non-EU visitors should check if their country has reciprocal arrangements.

Emergency Services

If you need to call any of the emergency services, speak clearly and the operator will understand you as they all speak a variety of languages. Few police officers speak English but all are happy to help tourists. The Hungarian word for police is *rendőrség*. Note that, while random ID checks are rare, you are legally required to carry a form of identification with you at all times. A photocopy of your passport will do.

Health

No specific vaccinations are required by visitors to Hungary, and pharmacies are ubiquitous: most open seven days a week. The Hungarian for pharmacy is *patika* or *gyógyszertár*, although you will see the German word *apotheke* in use as well. The 24-hour pharmacies closest to the city centre are Déli Gyógyszertár, opposite Déli Station in Buda, and Teréz Patika, near Oktogon metro station in Pest.

Budapest's hospitals are excellent, although doctors and nurses are relatively underpaid. Do tip them if you use their services. Foreigners will be given free medical care in an emergency, but you may be billed for ambulance services.

Hungarian dental treatment is good and cheap, and dental tourism a booming industry. If you urgently need a dentist, call **SOS Dental Services**, which operates Monday to Saturday.

Tap water is safe to drink in Hungary.

Personal Security

Budapest is a very safe city, and no particular precautions are needed. Avoid flashing large sums of money in public, don't get into an unmarked taxi, and don't talk to strange women on Váci utca.

There is almost no violent crime in Budapest, although petty crime is a problem. Backpackers are a favourite target for pickpockets, and the buses to and from Keleti Station are their haunts.

Disabled Travellers

Visitors with mobility issues will find that Budapest is reasonably well-equipped for their needs. Nearly all streets and pavements are sloped at junctions for wheelchair users. Most buses are accessible to the disabled, with entrances which can be lowered to pavement level. Many metro stations have also been made wheelchair-friendly, although the vast majority of trams remain inaccessible to all but the fittest, due to steep steps.

The **Hungarian Disabled Association** provides information on services such as transport, counselling and personal assistance.

Currency and Banking

Hungary's currency is the Forint (Ft). Coins in circulation are Ft5, Ft10, Ft20, Ft50, Ft100 and Ft200. Bank notes come in denominations of Ft500, Ft1,000, Ft2,000, Ft5,000, Ft10,000 and Ft20,000. It can be difficult to use notes of Ft10,000 and Ft20,000, especially in small stores, so it is advisable to have smaller notes on hand.

You can exchange foreign currency at banks, but they usually offer bad rates and have limited opening hours. Although independent exchange bureaux offer better rates, some have hidden costs and somewhat deceptive rate tables. Always check carefully the rates you are given.

The best and safest way to obtain local currency is with a credit or debit card from an ATM. Although the bank that issues the card may charge a small fee for each transaction, the exchange rate is closer to those on the foreign exchange market. Credit cards (Visa and Master-Card) are accepted just about everywhere, Diners Club and American Express less so.

Communication

Hungary boasts one of the fastest average internet speeds in the world. Visitors to Budapest will often find connections to be much quicker than those at home. The city is well covered with Wi-Fi hotspots, and almost all cafés, bars, restaurants and hotels provide it free of charge. Even Budapest airport provides free Wi-Fi for up to two hours.

To use your mobile device in Hungary, it will need to be equipped for GSM network frequencies 900/1800 MHz, UMTS/3G frequencies 2100 MHz and LTE/4G frequencies 800/1800/2600 MHz.

If you are a subscriber of any mobile operator in the EU, you can use your phone without extra roaming charges. Other visitors should consider buying a local SIM card in order to take advantage of local rates. Ask your home carrier for the unlock code to use a different SIM card/service. The three big Hungarian mobile networks, Vodafone, Telenor and Telekom, all offer pre-paid SIM cards, sold at most newsstands and kiosks, as well as mobile phone stores.

Hungarian mail is fast, efficient and reliable. Offices of Magyar Posta, the national mail service, usually open 7am–6pm. You can buy stamps from the post office and some newsstands. A standard letter weighing up to 20g or a postcard costs Ft340 within the EU, Ft395 to all other destinations. Most Hungarian post offices offer mail-holding (poste restante) services.

DIRECTORY

VISA INFORMATION
w konzuliszolgalat. kormany.hu/en

CONSULATES
UK
C 06 266 28 88
USA
C 06 475 44 00

TRAVEL SAFETY ADVICE
Australia
Department of Foreign Affairs and Trade
w dfat.gov.au
w smarttraveller.gov.au
UK
FCO
w gov.uk/foreign-travel-advice
USA
State Department
w travel.state.gov

EMERGENCY NUMBERS
C 112
Ambulance
C 104
Fire Service
C 105
Police
C 107

MEDICAL AID
Fönix S.O.S. Rt. Medical Service
C 06 200 01 00

SOS Dental Services
MAP D4 ■ VI, Király utca 14 (8am–8pm Mon–Sat) C 06 269 60 10

DISABLED TRAVELLERS
Hungarian Disabled Association
San Marco utca 76
C 06 250 90 13
w meosz.hu

BANKING
National Bank of Hungary
MAP C3 ■ 1054 Szabadság tér 8/9
C 06 428 26 00

Television and Radio

The state broadcaster, Magyar Televízió, operates the channels M1 and M2, of which the former has a foreign-language news programme. All other Hungarian television stations have no foreign-language programmes, and films are often dubbed rather than having sub-titles. However, most hotels also offer satellite and cable TV packages, which carry a wide variety of international channels, including CNN, BBC, ZDF, RTL and EuroNews. Music FM is Hungary's most popular radio station, playing a mix of local and international pop. It can be found in Budapest at 89.5FM.

Magazines and Newspapers

Unless you are able to read Hungarian, you will be limited to yesterday's news, as international newspapers arrive on the following day – *The Guardian* is an exception. The **Budapest Times** also has an English-language website. Foreign news-papers are available at most newsstands, but the best selection is at the **World Press House**. *Blikk* is the best-selling Hungarian daily tabloid newspaper, with *Népszabadság* the best-selling broadsheet.

Opening Hours

Banks are generally open 9am–4pm on weekdays, though opening hours can vary significantly. Shops keep long hours from Monday to Saturday (often 10am–8pm), with malls staying open until 10pm. Many shops, mainly the larger ones, are also open on Sundays, but they might close earlier than on other days. You should find plenty of small kiosks and a few hypermarkets selling basic necessities open 24 hours a day throughout the city.

Most museums and other main attractions are open every day, although some are shut on Mondays.

Time Difference

Budapest uses Central European time, in keeping with the majority of mainland Europe. This means it is two hours ahead of Greenwich Mean Time (GMT) in the summer and one hour ahead in winter.

Electrical Appliances

The electric current is 220 volts. Many electrical appliances, such as hair-dryers, have 110/220V transformers built in, so converters may be less of a concern, especially if you are coming from North America. Bring European adaptors with two round pins.

When to Go

Budapest's climate is one of extremes. Summers can be very hot, with temperatures soaring above 30°C (86°F) in July and August, while winter is often bitterly cold, and snow not uncommon. Spring is wet: May and June are the months with the heaviest rainfall. Late summer and autumn are perhaps the best times to visit the city.

Sources of Information

The Tourism Office of Budapest runs several **Tourinform** centres in Budapest. The main office is on Deák tér, and there are others at Liszt Ferenc tér, Buda Castle and the airport. They organize tours as well as offering maps and general information. The best listings magazine is the free monthly *Funzine Budapest*, published in English. It provides a good overview of what's going on in the city. You should find a copy at your hotel. Its website includes listings in English. Look out too for City Walks maps: these practical and informative maps help you explore the city's major attractions over 2- or 3-hour walking tours. They are updated every month and are available in most hotels in the city, free of charge.

Trips and Tours

Citytour runs two official hop-on, hop-off tours of Budapest: the Red Line (which leaves from József nádor tér) and the Yellow Line (from Erzsébet tér). Both depart every 30 minutes and take in the Castle District and central Pest, but otherwise follow different routes. The Red Line also visits Heroes' Square and Városliget Park, while the Yellow Line stops at Margaret Island and Gellért hegy. Both lines take around 2 hours to complete.

There is also a hop-on, hop-off boat boat, which travels from Petofi tér to Margaret Island and back. Tickets are valid on both bus lines and the boat, and are interchangeable as often as you like over a 24- or 48-hour period. Children under six travel for free.

A walking tour covering both Pest and Buda leaves from Andrassy út 22 (next to the Hungarian State Opera) at 10am each day. The tour is free, although you are expected to tip your guide.

Other free walking tours depart from Vörösmarty tér most days between 10am and 11am. Again, you should tip your guide.

Viator offers two very interesting tours – one of Communist Budapest, which visits many of the scenes of the 1956 revolution, and the other of Jewish Budapest. Both depart from Vörösmarty tér at 3:30pm each day.

Where to Eat

Budapest has a great range of places to eat at prices to suit all budgets, and food is very much part of the culture here. *Étterem* is the Hungarian word for restaurant, at which any kind of cuisine may be served. *Csárda* is a rather more subtle word, usually suggesting a folksy-type place serving traditional local food. A *vendéglő* is often (though not always) an informal bistro-style eatery, while a *cukrászda* is a patisserie.

There are plenty of places serving vegetarian food in Budapest. Most menus have vegetarian options, with tasty dishes such as *lescó* (pan-fried tomatoes and peppers) and vegetarian goulash.

When ordering meat, make sure that you state clearly how you want it cooked, otherwise it will be served on the burnt side of well done. Side dishes and vegetables are usually ordered separately. Hungarians also often order their desserts along with the rest of the meal.

As in other parts of Europe, a 10 per cent tip for good service is usually considered sufficient.

Children are generally welcome at all restaurants in the city, although very few have specific children's menus.

Where to Stay

Budapest has a broad range of places to stay, and is particularly blessed with luxury hotels. Many of the city's finest 19th-century palaces have now been converted to accommodate the more well-off visitor, but there is plenty of mid-range and budget accommodation too.

When deciding on accommodation, you should first choose the general location you want, which means deciding between Buda and Pest. In Pest, many hotels will often be only a few steps from many of the major tourist attractions, and from restaurants and nightlife. Those looking for more peace and quiet should head for Buda. Rates are reasonable by western European standards, and by booking via **Airbnb**, **Trivago**, **HRS** and **Booking.com** you can often grab bargains. It is not hard to find premium double rooms in outstanding locations for around Ft30,000. The average hotel room price in Budapest is Ft28,000.

DIRECTORY

DIRECTORY ENQUIRIES
199

NEWSPAPERS AND MAGAZINES

Budapest Times
budapesttimes.hu

Funzine Budapest
funzine.hu

World Press House
MAP C4 ■ V, Városház utca 3–5

SOURCES OF INFORMATION

Budapest
budapest.hu

Budapest Gay Guide
budapest.gay guide.net

Budapest Information
budapestinfo.hu

Hungary Tourism
hungary tourism.hu

Tourinform
MAP C4 ■ V, Sütő utca 2 (Deák tér)
06 438 80 80 (24 hrs)

TRIPS AND TOURS

City Tour
citytour.hu/en

Free Walking Tours
triptobudapest.hu
freebudapesttours.hu

Viator Tours
viator.com/budapest-walks

HOTEL BOOKINGS

Airbnb
airbnb.com

Booking.com
booking.com

HRS
hrs.com

Trivago
trivago.com

Places to Stay

PRICE CATEGORIES
For a standard, double room per night (with breakfast if included), taxes and extra charges.

F under Ft15,000 FF Ft15,000–30,000 FFF over Ft30,000

Luxury Hotels

Mamaison Andrássy Boutique Hotel
MAP M2 ▪ VI, Andrássy út 111 ▪ 06 462 21 00 ▪ www. mamaison.com ▪ FF
At the Andrássy, you will find all the elegance you could wish for. A Small Luxury Hotels of the World group member, it is set on the city's classiest boulevard. Rooms are superbly furnished, and it has a great restaurant.

Corinthia Grand Hotel Royal
MAP D3 ▪ VII, Erzsébet körút 43–9 ▪ 06 479 40 00 ▪ www.corinthia.com ▪ FFF
From its faithfully restored Secession façade to the exquisite atriums and foyer, the Grand Royal has been enticing discerning guests since 1896. With its central location, lavish rooms and first-class restaurants, this truly is a fabulous hotel.

Hilton Budapest
MAP G2 ▪ I, Hess András tér 1–3 ▪ 06 889 66 00 ▪ www.budapest.hilton. com ▪ FFF
The Hilton Budapest's imposing façade is one of the most instantly recognizable sights in the Castle District. It's a fantastic hotel, with well-furnished rooms, many of which have great Danube views.

Iberostar Grand
MAP K2 ▪ V, Október 6 utca 26 ▪ 06 354 30 50 ▪ www.iberostar.com ▪ FFF
Luxury and opulence near St Stephen's Cathedral. The spacious rooms are magnificently appointed, and complimented by a wide range of extras. There's also a superb spa.

Kempinski Hotel Corvinus Budapest
MAP L3 ▪ V, Erzsébet tér 7–8 ▪ 06 429 37 77 ▪ www.kempinski-budapest.com ▪ FFF
While the bold Kempinski Corvinus has a Modernist design on the outside, its interior offers lush furnishings, marble bathrooms and understated luxury. Most rooms overlook Elizabeth Square.

Nemzeti
MAP D4 ▪ VIII, József körút 4 ▪ 06 477 45 00 ▪ www.hotel-nemzeti-budapest.hu/en ▪ FFF
A Neo-Classical building this may be, but the comfortable rooms are strictly contemporary. The lobby and common areas are quite stunning, and the wine bar is a lively after-hours hangout.

Queen's Court
MAP D4 ▪ VII, Dob utca 63 ▪ 06 882 30 00 ▪ www.queenscourthotel budapest.com ▪ FFF
While not particularly attractive from the outside, within the Queen's Court hotel you will find nothing but the best, with the focus on superbly designed suites. It also boasts a luxurious indoor swimming pool and gym.

The Ritz-Carlton, Budapest
MAP L3 ▪ V, Erzsébet tér 9–10 ▪ 06 429 55 00 ▪ www.ritzcarlton.com ▪ FFF
A perfect combination of elegance and comfort, the Ritz-Carlton sits in a great location on Elizabeth Square. The listed building has been lovingly furnished in a clean, modern style.

Grand and Historic Hotels

Danubius Hotel Gellért
MAP L6 ▪ XI, Szent Gellért tér 1 ▪ 06 889 55 00 ▪ Dis. access ▪ www. danubiushotels.com/ gellert ▪ FF
Since World War I, the Gellért has played host to the rich and famous, who throng here to enjoy its Secession charm and thermal baths. The rooms are well kept and have great views over the Danube (see pp20–21).

Boscolo New York Palace Budapest
MAP D4 ▪ VII, Erzsébet körút 9–11 ▪ 06 886 61 11 ▪ www.boscolohotels. com ▪ FFF
At this unashamedly luxurious hotel, surfaces are rich in marble, bronze, steel and glass, and every en-suite has a marble bathtub. It is also home to the lavish New

York Café, one of the great literary hangouts of the 20th century *(see p98)*.

Buddha-Bar Hotel

MAP L4 ▪ V, Váci utca 34 ▪ 06 799 73 00 ▪ www.buddhabarhotel.hu ▪ FFF
This elegant five-star hotel, located in the Klotild Palace, has 102 rooms and a variety of suites. Buddha-Bar is equipped with the latest technology and luxurious amenities.

Hotel Continental Zara

MAP M4 ▪ VII, Dohány utca 42–4 ▪ 06 815 10 00 ▪ www.continentalhotelbudapest.com ▪ FFF
This building, with its stunning Art Nouveau façade, was a large bath house in the 1900s. It is now a business-oriented modern hotel with a roof garden and pool, plus a fitness centre.

Palace Zichy

MAP D5 ▪ VIII, Lőrinc pap tér 2 ▪ 06 235 40 00 ▪ www.hotel-palazzo-zichy.hu ▪ FFF
This Neu-Baroque mansion, built for Count Zichy, dates from 1899, and is now a luxurious hotel. Superb rooms are of a grand size, and the buffet breakfast is one of the city's best.

Boutique Hotels

Bohem

MAP L5 ▪ V, Molnár utca 35 ▪ 06 327 90 20 ▪ www.bohemarthotel.hu ▪ FF
This "art hotel" features the work of local artists. It's superbly located, just metres away from both the river and Váci utca, and room rates are more

than reasonable given the luxurious and stylish nature of the place.

Boutique Hotel Budapest

MAP L5 ▪ V, Só utca 6 ▪ 06 920 21 00 ▪ www.boutiquehotelbudapest.com ▪ FF
The somewhat minimalist and very contemporary interiors here are as cutting-edge as they come. There is a also a fantastic fusion restaurant.

Brody House

MAP M4 ▪ VIII, Bródy Sándor utca 10 ▪ 06 266 12 11 ▪ www.brodyhouse.com ▪ FF
This boutique hotel is attached to a private members' club. The communal area offers lovely views over the park beside the National Museum, and there is a well-stocked library. The staff are also able to give their visitors a great introduction to the city.

Parlament

MAP L1 ▪ V, Kálmán Imre utca 19 ▪ 06 374 60 00 ▪ www.parlament-hotel.hu ▪ FF
Behind its gorgeous exterior, the rooms here are distinguished by their smart wooden floors and simple yet elegant design. There's also a good spa centre, restaurant and bar.

Three Corners Boutique Hotel Bristol

MAP E4 ▪ VIII, Kenyér-mező utca 4 ▪ 06 799 11 00 ▪ www.threecorners.com ▪ FF
This hotel is spotlessly clean and surprisingly quiet, given its proximity

to the railway station. The staff seem eager to please, and the breakfast buffet is excellent.

Aria

MAP L3 ▪ V, Hercegprímás utca 5 ▪ 06 445 40 55 ▪ www.ariahotelbudapest.com ▪ FFF
Part of the exclusive Library Group, the Aria has a musical theme. The elegant interior courtyard here will take your breath away, as will the sublime rooms, all individually designed in quirky styles. Best of all is the rooftop bar, with stunning views.

Mamaison Residence Izabella Budapest

MAP D3 ▪ VI, Izabella utca 61 ▪ 06 475 59 00 ▪ Dis. access ▪ www.mamaison.com ▪ FFF
An apartment hotel with spacious one-, two- and three-bedroom apartments in a great location, just off Budapest's most exclusive street, Andrássy út. There is a 24-hour reception desk, security, parking and a health club.

Danube View Hotels

Buda Gold

MAP A5 ▪ I, Hegyalja út 14 ▪ 06 209 47 75 ▪ Dis. access ▪ www.goldhotel.hu ▪ FF
A splendid Buda hotel, located a short walk from the Citadella. Housed in a great building, complete with a tower, it was only built in 1997. Rooms have cherry-wood parquet floors, and most have great views over the Danube or the Buda Hills. The tower rooms, though pricey, are the best.

Hotel Victoria

MAP H2 ▪ I, Bem rakpart 11 ▪ 06 457 80 80 ▪ www.victoria.hu ▪ FF

Located beneath Buda Castle on the Danube embankment, this charming, mid-range hotel offers 27 spacious, well-equipped rooms, all with fantastic river views. The staff are knowledgeable and helpful.

Lánchíd 19

MAP J4 ▪ I, Lánchíd utca 19 ▪ 06 457 12 00 ▪ www.lanchid19hotel.com ▪ FF

Situated on the Buda embankment, this modern "design hotel" features a unique glass façade, which changes colour during the evening. There are many stylish design touches inside, too. Rooms are large, equipped with lots of high-tech gizmos, and most have city views. The penthouse suites are simply dazzling.

art'otel

MAP H1 ▪ I, Bem rakpart 16–19 ▪ 06 487 94 87 ▪ Dis. access ▪ www.artotels.com ▪ FFF

Situated in a sublime Neo-Baroque building on the banks of the Danube, this is a truly contemporary hotel, inspired by modern art and design. Works by American artist Donald Sultan are on display, and the art concept covers everything from the carpets to the cutlery.

Budapest Marriott

MAP K4 ▪ V, Apáczai Csere János utca 4 ▪ 06 486 50 00 ▪ www.marriott.com/budhu ▪ FFF

The first of the five-star hotels in Budapest, the Marriott dates from 1969, and its Modernist

architecture still stands out on the banks of the Danube. All the rooms benefit from stunning views.

Four Seasons Hotel Gresham Palace

MAP K3 ▪ V, Széchenyi István tér 5–6 ▪ 06 268 60 00 ▪ Dis. access ▪ www.fourseasons.com ▪ FFF

The cost of staying at the city's most expensive hotel becomes insignificant as soon as you step into the foyer – it's a wonder of modern design in a classic setting. A Secession landmark, the Gresham Palace offers splendid service and views of the Chain Bridge, Danube and the Buda Hills (see p83).

Intercontinental

MAP K3 ▪ V, Apáczai Csere János utca 12–14 ▪ 06 327 63 33 ▪ www.budapest.intercontinental.com ▪ FFF

Spacious rooms with windows overlooking the Danube are the main draw of this perennially popular hotel. The public reception areas are welcoming, and the hotel's Corso restaurant gets excellent reviews, especially for the lavish Sunday brunch buffet.

Sofitel Budapest Chain Bridge

MAP K3 ▪ V, Széchenyi István tér 2 ▪ 06 266 12 34 ▪ www.sofitel.com ▪ FFF

In a superb location on Széchenyi István tér with views of the Danube and the Royal Palace, this hotel offers bright rooms with large bay windows. The Paris-Budapest Café, with its innovative cuisine, is a great place to relax.

Mid-Range and Apart-Hotels

Dominika Apartman Hotel

MAP N2 ▪ XII, Lidérc utca 13 ▪ 06 246 00 62 ▪ Dis. access ▪ No air conditioning ▪ www.dominikahotel.hu ▪ F

At the cheap end of the apartment sector, these superb apartments are housed inside a delightful guesthouse in a leafy Budapest suburb. There's a delightful terrace and even a swimming pool at the back of the building.

Carlton Hotel

MAP H3 ▪ I, Apor Péter utca 3 ▪ 06 224 09 99 ▪ www.carltonhotel.hu ▪ FF

The austere-looking Carlton is a good mid-range hotel. Decor is rather basic, but all 95 rooms are comfortable and have air conditioning. An excellent buffet breakfast is included in the price of your room.

Ibis Centrum

MAP M5 ▪ IX, Ráday utca 6 ▪ 06 456 41 00 ▪ Dis. access ▪ www.ibis.com ▪ FF

Part of the Ibis chain, which offers a decent level of accommodation at low prices. It's located on one of the busiest streets in town, but rooms are soundproofed from the noise below. There's a lovely garden patio.

Locust Tree Apartments

MAP D4 ▪ VII, Akacfa utca 12 ▪ 0670 394 26 51 ▪ www.locusttreeapartments.com ▪ FF

Modern needn't mean soulless. This relaxed

apartment hotel, on a busy street full of clubs, bars and cafés, offers cable TV, tea, coffee and a laundry service – all at a fair price.

Manzárd Panzió

MAP F6 ▪ Bláthy Ottó utca 21▪ 06 210 41 41 ▪ www.manzardpanzio. com ▪ FF

Located in a quiet residential area of downtown Budapest, the Manzard Panzió is a charming if simple hotel. It has a large garden, provides free Wi-Fi access and arranges barbecue and goulash parties.

Sissi

MAP P2 ▪ IX, Angyal utca 33 ▪ 06 215 00 82 ▪ Dis. access ▪ www. hotelsissi.hu ▪ FF

Named after Elizabeth (Erzsébet) – the wife of Emperor Franz József II – who was known to her friends as Sissi, this hotel is worthy of her name. It is a charming place with smart interiors and 44 large rooms, some of which have balconies. Several rooms are set aside as non-smoking.

City Gardens Apartment Hotel

MAP M1 ▪ VI, Ó utca 43–49 ▪ 0620 285 08 07 ▪ www.citygardens budapest.com ▪ FFF

All the mod cons you need – including a DVD library, tea- and coffee-making facilities and free Wi-Fi – make these apartments a viable alternative to traditional hotels. The building also has a gym and sauna for guests to use. Airport transfers can be arranged when booking.

Cheap Sleeps

Boat Hostel Fortuna

MAP C1 ▪ XIII, Szent István Park, Alsó rakpart ▪ 06 288 81 00 ▪ www. fortunahajo.hu ▪ F

Most of this boat is part of a rather fine hotel, but there are also dorm rooms in the hull, which market themselves as a hostel. These are cheaper, though more crowded, than the hotel rooms.

Carpe Noctem Vitae Hostel

MAP D4 ▪ VII, Erzsébet körút 50 ▪ 0670 670 03 87 ▪ www.budapestparty hostels.com ▪ F

A lively hostel, which offers a range of different sized dorms as well as private rooms. Great staff, plus immaculately clean bathrooms and one of the best party atmospheres in the city. Not for those looking for a quite time.

easyHotel Budapest Oktogon

MAP M1 ▪ VI, Eötvös utca 25/a ▪ www.easyhotel. com ▪ F

Situated in historic Pest, at the crossroads of Andrássy út and Oktogon, this hotel has a location that is hard to beat. The simple, clean rooms have private bathrooms and, for a fee, there is Wi-Fi and the use of a TV.

Full Moon Hostel

MAP C2 ▪ V, Szent István körút 11 ▪ 06 792 90 45 ▪ www.fullmoonhostel. com ▪ F

Bright and colourful, with huge portraits of 1960s rock stars at every turn, this is a vibrant, late-night hostel. It offers decent accommodation in an

assortment of options, including private rooms.

Gaia Hostel

MAP L4 ▪ V, Kossuth Lajos utca 17 ▪ 0630 957 89 57 ▪ F

There is a huge range of rooms here, from rather elegant private doubles to far more simple dorms. In a great location downtown, it is just a few metres from the metro.

The Groove

MAP C2 ▪ XIII, Szent István körút 16 ▪ 06 786 80 38 ▪ www.groove hostel.hu ▪ F

A friendly hostel with great staff in a decent location close to just about everything. There are four-, six- and eight-person dorms, as well as a private double. The common room gets lively during the evening.

Shantee House

MAP N2 ▪ XI,Takács Menyhért utca 33 ▪ 06 385 89 46 ▪ www.back packbudapest.com ▪ F

Popular with young backpackers, this guest-house is always buzzing. There's a courtyard, and while the rooms are basic, they are impeccably clean and have fresh linen daily. Air conditioning is not offered in the rooms.

Fifteen Boutique Hostel

MAP A3 ▪ XII, Széll Kálmán tér 15 ▪ 06 794 97 69 ▪ www.facebook. com/budapestfifteen ▪ FF

A cut above your average hostel. The bathrooms here would pass in many five-star hotels. Minutes from the Castle District, it is ideal for sightseeing, less so for nightlife.

For a key to hotel price categories see p114

General Index

Acknowledgments

Author

A linguist by training, Craig Turp has spent the majority of his adult life studying and writing about the languages and peoples of Central and Eastern Europe. He has written a number of guide books to the region, and is a key member of the team that publishes the *In Your Pocket* series of independent, locally produced city guides. He lives in Bucharest, Romania.

Publishing Director Georgina Dee

Publisher Vivien Antwi

Design Director Phil Ormerod

Editorial Michelle Crane, Rachel Fox, Fay Franklin, Priyanka Kumar, Sally Schafer, Hollie Teague, Sophie Wright

Design Tessa Bindloss, Richard Czapnik, Marisa Renzullo Stuti Tiwari

Commissioned Photography Demetrio Carrasco, Rough Guides/Eddie Gerald

Picture Research Ellen Root, Lucy Sienkowska, Rituraj Singh

Cartography Subhashree Bharti, Uma Bhattacharya, James Macdonald, Casper Morris

DTP Jason Little, Azeem Siddiqui

Production Che Creasey

Factchecker Krisztián R. Hildebrand

Proofreader Susanne Hillen

Indexer Helen Peters

Picture Credits

The publisher would like to thank the following for their kind permission to reproduce their photographs:
Key: a-above; b-below/bottom; c-centre; f-far; l-left; r-right; t-top

123RF.com: asafeliason 81cra; Michal Bednarek 94cla; Alex Tihonov 96b.

4Corners: Massimo Borchi 61cl; SIME/Davide Erbetta 60tl; Richard Taylor 1, 24-5.

Restaurant Alabárdos: 55cla.

Alamy Stock Photo: AD Photo 4clb; age fotostock/Renaud Visage 3tl, 66-7; Agencia Fotograficzna Caro/Muhs 58cl; Alpineguide 31br; Eyal Bartov 91cl; Blend Images/Spaces Images 11cr; Danita Delimont/Jim Engelbrecht 42cl; Zoltan Fabian 77cla; Peter Forsberg 4cla, 89cra; funkyfood London - Paul Williams 100cla; imageBROKER/Hermann Dobler 72br; Images-Europa 76tl; incamerastock 3tr, 106-7; Interfoto/Fine Arts 88cra; JTB MEDIA CREATION, Inc./JTB Photo 37tl, /UIG 96tl; John Kellerman 4t, 11tl, 11crb, 17tl, 69cra; 75br, 76b, 89bl, 90cra, Andriy Kravchenko 18-9; Motion/Horizon Images 50clb; B. O'Kane 20bc; Bernard O'Kane 18c;

Mo Peerbacus 48br, 52br, 61tr; Photicon 70b; SFM GM WORLD 102tl; Anna Todero 59br; Endless Travel 43ll; TravelCollection 47cl; TravelCollection/Darshana Borges 64cla; Zoonar GmbH/Heinz Leitner 55tr.

Arany Kaviár Étterem: 73cr.

Asztalka Cukrászda : 79cb.

AWL Images: Ken Scicluna 4cl.

Baraka: Zsolt Batar 54br.

The Big Fish: Barnabas Imre 99bl.

Borbíróság Étterem: 93cr.

Boscolo Budapest: New York Café 57b, 98t.

Boutiq'Bar: 59cl.

Bridgeman Images: The Stapleton Collection/ Private Collection 40t.

Budai Gesztenye és: 105cr.

Budapest Wine Festival: Zsolt Szigetvary 63cl.

Corbis: Atlantide Phototravel/ Massimo Borchi 18br, 53crb, 83cla; JAI/Neil Farrin 19tl; Leemage 41br; Ottochrome/Nathan Benn 36br; Sylvain Sonnet 15tr, 20cl, 45tl; Sygma/ Bernard Bisson 41cl; Xinhua/Attila Volgyi 53tl.

Danubius Hotel Gellért: 20-1c,21cr,79cra; Café Astoria 92cla.

Doblo: 56tr, 92br.

Dreamstime.com: Alessandro0770 11bc; Alinamd 38-9c; Anilah 36-7; Artzzz 61br; Asafta 59tl; Michal Bednarek 4b; Belizar 11tr; Ivan Vander Biesen 2tl, 8-9; Bimserd 10bl; Boggy 10cla,13br; Bramble100 37bc; Ccat82 23l; Ciolca 74tl; Demerzel21 10clb, 80tl; Chris Dorney 4cra, 95br; Razvan Ionut Dragomirescu 49r; Dziewul 81b; Shchipkova Elena 2tr, 38-9b, 95cla; Stefano Ember 18cla; Emicristea 29bl; Empipe 47tr; Aaron Frutman 4crb; Igorp1976 60br; Laraclarence 22cr; Ihsin Liu 63br; Mikhail Markovskiy 16bc, 48t; Milosk50 12-3; Roland Nagy 78b; Tatiana Savvateeva 51b, 101br; Scanrail 16cl, 82t; Stephan Scherhag 65br; Sgar80 16-7; Peter Spirer 13ca; Tartalia 30cla; Tomas1111 7tr,10c; Tupungato 103cl; Ferenc Ungor 36cla; Svetlana Voronina 47br; Wavemovies 37c, 44b; Hilda Weges 30-1, 65t; Noppasin Wongchum 6tl, 69b, 86-7.

Ethnographical Museum: 43c.

Four Seasons Hotels and Resorts - Gresham Palace: 85cr

Gerbeaud Gasztronomia Ltd: 54tl, 54c, 57tr.

Getty Images: Bloomberg/Akos Stiller 50tr; DEA/S. Vannini 30rcb.

Hungarian Arts & Crafts Festival: 62br.

Hungarian National Assembly: 15bl; Mark Mervai 12bl.

Hungarian National Museum: 34tr, 34cla,34br, 35tl, 35crb.

Hungarian State Opera: Attila Juha 32cla; Attila Juhasz 32-3, 33tl; Attila Nagy 32br; 82br.

Kassák Museum: 104cla.

Magnolia Day Spa: 46tr.

Mary Evans Picture Library: 40bl.

Memories of Hungary: 59cr.

Miniversum: 52cl.

Museum of Fine Arts Budapest: Gyula Benczúr *The Recapture of Buda Castle* 1896 26cl; Károly Ferenczy *Birdsong* 1667 27tc; Lajos Gulácsy *The Garden of the Magician* 1906-1907/Fehér Katalin 29c; Master MS *The Visitation* 1500-1510 26tr; Mihály Munkácsy *The Yawning Apprentice* 1869/Mester Tibor 26crb; József Rippl-Rónai *Woman in a White-Spotted Dress* 1898 28tc; József Rippl-Rónai *The Manor House at Körtvelyes* 1907/Berényi Zsuzsa 28bl; János Vaszary *Fancy Dress Ball* 1907 28crb.

Oscar American Cocktail Bar: 72cla.

Ötkert: Soós Bertalan 84cl.

Rex by Shutterstock: Colorsport 102br; N 51cr.

Robert Harding Picture Library: Stuart Black 70tl; Peter Erik Forsberg 71cla; Eduardo Grund 97cl; Mel Longhurst 43br; Carlo Morucchio 45cr; Ingolf Pompe 90bl.

SuperStock: age fotostock/Domingo Leiva Nicolas 10crb; imageBROKER 22cla, / Matthias Hauser 23br.

Sziget: Sa ándor Csudai 62t.

Szimpla Kert: 56cl.

Törley Museum: 101cla.

Wekerle Community Association: Miklós; dr.Toldy 104br.

Cover
Front and spine: **Getty Images:** Romeo Reidl
Back: **Dreamstime.com:** Rudi1976.

Pull Out Map Cover
Getty Images: Romeo Reidl.

All other images © Dorling Kindersley
For further information see:
www.dkimages.com

As a guide to abbreviations in visitor information blocks: **Adm** = admission charge; **DA** = disabled access; **D** = dinner; **L** = lunch.

Penguin
Random
House

Printed and bound in China

First published in Great Britain in 2006
by Dorling Kindersley Limited
80 Strand, London WC2R 0RL

Copyright 2006, 2017 © Dorling
Kindersley Limited

A Penguin Random House Company

16 17 18 19 10 9 8 7 6 5 4 3 2 1

**Reprinted with revisions 2008, 2010,
2012, 2014, 2017**

ISBN 978 0 24126 556 7

MIX
Paper from
responsible sources
FSC FSC™ C018179
www.fsc.org

SPECIAL EDITIONS OF DK TRAVEL GUIDES

DK Travel Guides can be purchased in bulk quantities at discounted prices for use in promotions or as premiums. We are also able to offer special editions and personalized jackets, corporate imprints, and excerpts from all of our books, tailored specifically to meet your own needs.

To find out more, please contact:

in the US
specialsales@dk.com

in the UK
travelguides@uk.dk.com

in Canada
specialmarkets@dk.com

in Australia
**penguincorporatesales@
penguinrandomhouse.com.au**

Phrase Book

In an Emergency

Help!	Segítség!	shegeetshayg!
Stop!	Stop!	shtop!
Call a doctor	Hívjon orvost!	heevyon orvosht!
Call an ambulance	Hívjon mentőt!	heevyon menturt
Call the police	Hívja a rendőrséget	heevya a rendur shayget
Call the fire department	Hívja a tűzoltókat!	heevya a tewzoltowkot!
Where is the nearest telephone?	Hol van a legközelebbi telefon?	hol von uh legkurze-lebbi telefon?
Where is the nearest hospital?	Hol van a legközelebbi kórház?	hol von a leg-kurze-lebbi koorhahz?

Communications Essentials

Yes/No	Igen/Nem	igen/nem
Please (offering)	Tessék	teshayk
Please (asking)	Kérem	kayrem
Thank you	Köszönöm	kurssurnurm
No, thank you	Köszönöm nem	kurssurnurm nem
Excuse me, please	Bocsánatot kérek	bochanutot kayrek
Hello	Jó napot	yow nopot
Goodbye	Viszontlátásra	vissont-latashruh
What?	Mi?	mi?
When?	Mikor?	mikor?
Why?	Miért?	miayrt?
Where?	Hol?	hol?

Useful Phrases

How are you?	Hogy van?	hod-yuh vun?
Very well, thank you	köszönöm nagyon jól	kurssurnurm nojjon yowl
Pleased to meet you	Örülök hogy megismerhettem	ur-rewlurk hod-yuh megish-merhettem
Where can I get…?	Hol kaphatok …-t?	hol kuphutok …-t?
How do you get to?	Hogy lehet …-ba eljutni?	hod-yuh lehet …-buh el-yootni?
Do you speak English?	Beszél angolul?	bessayl ungolool?
I can't speak Hungarian	Nem beszélek magyarul	nem bessaylek mud-yarool
I don't understand	Nem értem	nem ayrtem
Can you help me?	Kérhetem a segítségét?	kayrhetem uh sheg-eechaygayt
Please speak slowly	Tessék lassabban beszélni	teshayk lushubbun bessaylni
Sorry!	Elnézést!	elnayzaysht!

Useful Words

big	nagy	noj
small	kicsi	kichi
hot	forró	forow
cold	hideg	hideg
good	jó	yow
bad	rossz	ross
open	nyitva	nyitva
closed	zárva	zarva
left	bal	bol
right	jobb	yob
entrance	bejárat	beh-yarut
exit	kijárat	ki-yarut

toilet	WC	vaytsay
free/unoccupied	szabad	sobbod
free/no charge	ingyen	injen

Making a Telephone Call

Can I call abroad from here?	Telefonálhatok innen külföldre?	telefonalhutok inen kewlfurldreh?
Could I leave a message?	Hagyhatnék egy üzenetet?	hud-yuhutnayk ed-yuh ewzenetet?
Hold on	Várjon!	vahr-yon!

Shopping

How much is this?	Ez mennyibe kerül?	ez menn-yibeh kerewl?
Do you have…?	Kapható önöknél…?	kuphutaw urnurknayl?
Do you take credit cards?	Elfogadják a hitelkártyákat?	elfogud-yak uh hitelkart-yakut?
What time do you open/ close?	Hánykor nyitnak/ zárnak?	Hahn kor nyitnak/ zárnak?
this one	ez	ez
expensive	drága	drahga
cheap	olcsó	olchow
size	méret	mayret
white	fehér	feheer
black	fekete	feketeh
red	piros	pirosh
yellow	sárga	sharga
green	zöld	zurld
blue	kék	cake
brown	barna	borna

Types of Shop

antiques dealer	régiségkereskedő	ray-gee-shayg-kereshk-kedur
bank	bank	bonk
bookshop	könyvesbolt	kurn-yuveshbolt
cake shop	cukrászda	tsookrassduh
chemist	patika	putikuh
department store	áruház	aroo-haz
florist	virágüzlet	virag-ewzlet
food store	élelmiszerbolt	ail-ell-miss-er
market	piac	pi-uts
newsagent	újságos	oo-yushagosh
post office	postahivatal	poshta-hivatal
shoe shop	cipőbolt	tsipurbolt
souvenir shop	ajándékbolt	uy-yandaykbolt
tobacconist	trafik	trafik
travel agent	utazási iroda	ootuzashi iroduh

Staying in a Hotel

Have you any vacancies?	Van kiadó szobájuk?	vun ki-udaw soba-yook?
double room with double bed	francia-ágyas szoba	frontsia-ahjosh sobuh
twin room	kétágyas szoba	kaytad-yush sobuh
single room	egyágyas szoba	ed-yad-yush sobuh
room with a bath/shower	fürdőszobás/ zuhanyzós szoba	fewrdur-sobahsh/zoo-honzahsh soba
porter	portás	purtuhsh
key	kulcs	koolch
I have a reservation	Foglaltam egy szobát	foglultum ed-yuh sobat

Sightseeing

bus	autóbusz	*owtawbooss*
tram	villamos	*villumosh*
train	vonat	*vonut*
underground	metró	*metraw*
bus stop	buszmegálló	*booss megallaw*
art gallery	képcsarnok	*kayp-chornok*
palace	palota	*polola*
church	templom	*templom*
garden	kert	*kert*
library	könyvtár	*kurnvtar*
museum	múzeum	*moozayoom*
tourist information	túristahivatal	*toorishta-hivotol*
closed for public holiday	ünnepnap zárva	*ewn-nepnap zarva*

Eating Out

A table for… please	Egy asztalt szeretnék… személyre	*ed-yuh usstult seretnayk… semayreh*
I want to reserve a table	Szeretnékegy asztalt foglalni	*seretnayk ed-yuh usstult foglolni*
The bill please	Kérem a számlát	*kayrem uh samlat*
I am a vegetarian	Vegetariánnus vagyok	*vegetariahnoosh vojok*
I'd like…	Szeretnék egy…-t	*seret nayk ed-yuh…-t*
waiter/ waitress	pincér/ pincérnő	*pintsayr/ pintsaymur*
menu	étlap	*aytlup*
wine list	borlap	*bohrlup*
drinks menu	itallap	*itallup*
glass	pohár	*pohar*
bottle	üveg	*ewveg*
knife	kés	*kaysh*
fork	villa	*villuh*
spoon	kanál	*kunal*
breakfast	reggeli	*reg-geli*
lunch	ebéd	*ebayd*
dinner	vacsora	*vochora*
main courses	főételek	*fur-aytelek*
starters	előételek	*elur-aytelek*
desserts	desszertek	*dess-air-tekh*
rare	angolosan	*ongoloshan*
well done	átsütve	*ahtshewtveh*

Menu Decoder

ásványvíz	*ahshvahnveez*	mineral water
bárány	*bahrahn*	lamb
bors	*borsh*	pepper
csirke	*cheerkeh*	chicken
csokoládé	*chokolahday*	chocolate
cukor	*tsookor*	sugar
ecet	*etset*	vinegar
fagylalt	*fodyuhloot*	ice cream
fehérbor	*feheerbor*	white wine
fokhagyma	*fokhodyuhma*	garlic
főtt	*furt*	boiled
gomba	*gomba*	mushrooms
gyümölcs	*dyewmurlch*	fruit
gyümölcslé	*dyewmurlch-lay*	fruit juice
hagyma	*hojma*	onions
hal	*hol*	fish
hús	*hoosh*	meat
kávé	*kavay*	coffee
kenyér	*ken-yeer*	bread
krumpli	*kroompli*	potatoes
kolbász	*kolbahss*	sausage
leves	*levesh*	soup
marha	*marha*	beef
mustár	*mooshtahr*	mustard
paradicsom	*porodichom*	tomatoes
párolt	*pahrolt*	steamed
rizs	*rizh*	rice
bifsztek	*bifstek*	steak
roston	*roshton*	grilled
sajt	*shoyt*	cheese
saláta	*sholahta*	salad
sertéshús	*shertaysh-hoosh*	pork
só	*shaw*	salt
sonka	*shonka*	ham
sör	*shur*	beer
sült	*shewlt*	fried/roasted
sült burgonya	*shewlt boorgonya*	chips
sütemény	*shewtemayn-yuh*	cake, pastry
tea	*tay-uh*	tea
tej	*tay*	milk
tejszín	*taysseen*	cream
tengeri hal	*tengeri hol*	sea fish
tojás	*toyahsh*	egg
vörösbor	*vur-rurshbor*	red wine
zsemle	*zhemleh*	roll
zsemlegom-bóc	*zhemlehgom-bowts*	dumplings

Numbers

0	nulla	*noolluh*
1	egy	*ed-yuh*
2	kettő, két	*kettur, kayt*
3	három	*harom*
4	négy	*nayd-yuh*
5	öt	*urt*
6	hat	*hut*
7	hét	*hayt*
8	nyolc	*n-yolts*
9	kilenc	*kilents*
10	tíz	*teez*
11	tizenegy	*tizened-yuh*
12	tizenkettő	*tizenkettur*
13	tizenhárom	*tizenharom*
14	tizennégy	*tizen-nayd-yuh*
15	tizenöt	*tizenurt*
16	tizenhat	*tizenhut*
17	tizenhét	*tizenhayt*
18	tizennyolc	*tizenn-yolts*
19	tizenkilenc	*tizenkilents*
20	húsz	*hooss*
30	harminc	*hurmints*
40	negyven	*ned-yuven*
50	ötven	*urtven*
60	hatvan	*hutvun*
70	hetven	*hetven*
80	nyolcvan	*n-yoltsvun*
90	kilencven	*kilentsven*
100	száz	*saz*
1,000	ezer	*ezer*
10,000	tízezer	*teezezer*
1,000,000	millió	*milliaw*

Time

one minute	egy perc	*ed-yuh perts*
hour	óra	*awruh*
half an hour	félóra	*faylawruh*
Sunday	vasárnap	*vushamap*
Monday	hétfő	*haytfur*
Tuesday	kedd	*kedd*
Wednesday	szerda	*serduh*
Thursday	csütörtök	*chewturturk*
Friday	péntek	*payntek*
Saturday	szombat	*sombut*

Selected Budapest Street Index